DAVINA'S

Kitchen Favourites

DAVINA'S

Kitchen

Favourites

Amazing sugar-free, no-fuss recipes
to enjoy together

Davina McCall

SEVEN DIALS

Contents

Hi Everyone

It's Davina again. Welcome to my kitchen – my fave place! A place of chat, laughter, heart-to-hearts and lots and lots of cooking!!!!

I've got to a stage in life now where I want to concentrate on the things that really matter. For me that's being with the ones I love and feeding them satisfying and healthy food.

This recipe collection comes from the heart. It's about family cooking and that can include everyone and anyone we love – relatives, friends or a neighbour who lives on their own and may be fed up of cooking meals for one.

These recipes are the ones I make because they're simple. They don't have lots of ingredients or cooking stages – and there's as little washing up as possible, honest!

Now the healthy bit . . .

It's a tricky word 'healthy', but if you tune out the nonsense and the fad diets and pseudo-science, there are clear nutritional rules that will help us all live longer and live better. From giving the kids the best start in life to making sure our beloved grannies and grandpas are getting the nutrients they need to stay strong and trim, the message is the same.

And that message is clear: no refined sugar and fewer processed foods.

So this is what DAVINA'S KITCHEN FAVOURITES is all about: great food for any age. Food that will feed our bodies, minds and souls and won't take too long or much effort to cook.

Share the love, show you care and get ready to do some cooking.

#sharethelove

Is sugar free, sugar free??

It almost feels like I'm talking about a different person but a few years ago I used to pile loads of sugar into my tea, hunt chocolate down in the house like the Crystal Maze and turn to the biscuit tin whenever I felt stressed. I loved my food and I loved cooking but I wasn't always sure what the best advice to follow was. Should I eat carbs or not? Low-fat foods – yes or no? I didn't want to do anything crazy, I wanted a good sensible healthy way of eating, with fewer sweet things and no added sugar.

When I started working on my own recipe books, I met some wonderful cooks and nutritional experts. I learned that healthy eating wasn't all about going for the latest weird magic ingredient but simply about eating a wide variety of fresh food, making sure I had plenty of fruit and vegetables, and choosing unrefined carbs instead of the white stuff.

Most importantly, I started going 'sugar free' – that is, avoiding adding sugar to my food. That has now extended to the cooking I do for family and friends. My kitchen is free from added sugar – white, brown, all sorts, except a little maple syrup and honey.

No more cravings

I used to think I needed sugar for energy but I've steered clear of sugar for ages now and I've got more energy than ever before – AND I've just hit 50!

I no longer crave sugar like I used to but once in a while I like to make a little something sweet that's as guilt-free as possible. I enjoy these treats – but not too often. At first I used to relax the rules a bit when I was entertaining and I sometimes made a sugary cake or dessert. Now there's NO sugar in my cupboard and I find everyone is more than happy with the puddings and bakes in this and my other books. They include some maple syrup or honey where necessary or rely on just the yummy natural sweetness of fruit and vegetables.

And yes – maple syrup and honey are sugars and the body reacts to them in the same way as it does to the white stuff, but they are less processed and closer to their natural state. They are sweeter too so I find I need less of them in my recipes. Win, win. Having that discipline of no added sugar has really helped me reduce my sweet tooth.

I always check labels for the hidden sugar in foods. Canned soups, bottled sauces, fruit yoghurts and ready meals often contain far more sugar than we realise so they're best avoided. I've taken these things off my shopping lists.

As well as avoiding added sugar in my food I've also cut out refined white carbs. We need carbs for energy and for our bodies to work properly but we really do not need refined carbohydrates like white bread, white pasta and white rice. They act just like sugar in our bodies. They are digested quickly, giving us a rush of energy and a blood sugar spike. Then we crash, feel more hungry than ever and want more food. Blood sugar is more of a concern than ever before, as so many people struggle with type 2 diabetes.

Complex carbs, though, such as vegetables, pulses and wholegrains, are digested much more slowly. They are packed with vitamins and minerals as well as fibre (more about that later!). They keep us feeling fuller for longer and help to maintain steady blood sugar.

DAVINA'S KITCHEN RULES

You know me – I'm not a nutritionist but I have talked to the experts and I want to share what they've taught me. Along with my exercise routines, their rules have worked to keep me trim and happy and helped me feed everyone great food. I've discovered some cheats along the way too that mean I don't dread the chore of cooking . . . I love it! This is what I've learned in a nutshell and the way my family eats now. I promise you there is no compromise in taste or satisfaction.

- **We've stopped adding refined sugar to drinks and food.**

- **We avoid processed foods and foods with 'hidden sugar'.**

- **We've cut out refined white carbohydrates such as white flour, white rice and white pasta.**

- **We eat loads of fresh vegetables and fruit, some meat and fish, pulses, eggs and some dairy.**

- **We opt for brown rice, brown pasta and wholemeal or spelt flour.**

- **We make puddings and cakes with naturally sweet ingredients such as fruit and veg or for a treat, we add some maple syrup or honey.**

Time is sooooo precious

My kitchen habits have changed over the years, and now I like to know exactly what I'm eating – that means, no ready meals. The great news is that this doesn't have to mean that cooking is a chore or recipes have to take ages to put together. You'll find plenty of recipes in this book that can be prepared in minutes and don't take too long to cook either. Others do need a bit more time so save those for weekends or when you feel like spending longer in the kitchen.

Working, caring, parenting, running around . . . it's FRAZZLING! So many of us are time poor these days and finding time to cook can be hard, which means that processed foods sometimes offer a tempting solution. But they're expensive and ultimately not great for our health or our waistlines. Throwing together healthy meals is much easier if you have the right ingredients in your fridge, freezer and cupboards, such as cans of beans, frozen veg and packets of lentils, and doesn't have to take ages.

I like to do some batch cooking too. I make a big pot of tomato sauce or baked beans or soup and stash some in the freezer for those nights when I'm extra rushed. And I've found that having some bags of cooked chickpeas, beans and even quinoa in the freezer is a huge help. They defrost quickly and make putting together a quick meal super easy.

Count them on your fingers – only 10 ingredients or less per recipe!

Are you put off by the long, long recipes with long, long ingredients lists? I am – so I've simplified everything here but with no cost to taste, flavour or satisfaction.

In this book, we've kept the recipes to 10 ingredients (very occasionally 11 or 12) but they're still just as amaaaazing. We felt that was about the right number for making sure the dishes are yummy and interesting but not too much of a faff. All the ingredients are things you will find in the supermarket – there may be a few less familiar items but nothing crazy you have to search for on the internet.

BTW, we don't include salt, pepper, olive or vegetable oil in the ingredients lists so check your stocks of those before starting to cook.

Sitting round the table

Food isn't just about health and nutrition. It's a social thing. I like to eat with friends. I like to share meals with my family and I love to cook for people when I can. There's really nothing nicer than sitting round the table with the people you love. We're all so busy and we have to work long hours but as often as possible it's so important for the family to sit down together to eat, talk and share the events of the day. We try to sit down for dinner and for Sunday roasts – my fave times.

It's not always easy these days, I know, with parents working or grown-up kids coming in at all hours, but children learn from what they see so it's good for them to see you eating well, getting your five a day and avoiding junk and refined sugar. They accept that it is the normal thing to do and that food is a pleasure as well as fuel for the body. Start them young and get them into the habit of eating a wide variety of foods and being willing to try things.

My three have been through the fussy eating stage and we're well out on the other side now but I know it can get frustrating. Cooking with kids is a messy joy, but I encouraged mine to join in the preparation of the meal – peeling and podding and stirring – and found they were more likely to eat the results. You just have to let go of your tidy kitchen!

To up everyone's veg intake, I've got into the habit of including extra vegetables in my cooking – throw a handful of peas into your spaghetti sauce or add a few spoonfuls of sweetcorn to a shepherd's pie. On page 120 of this book you'll find a great Italian-style meat sauce made with half lentils and half meat, making it good for your body and your budget.

Going veggie

Primary school age children generally love to help in the kitchen and view it all as a great game but things can get trickier when they hit the teenage years. If your family aren't vegetarian already, your son or daughter may announce one day that he or she wants to go veggie. Great – support their decision. It's a really healthy way of eating as it means more veggies, but just help them make sure they are not missing out on essential nutrients such as iron and calcium. Make the point that being a vegetarian isn't just about not eating meat but making sure you fill your protein needs in other ways and get a good balanced diet.

Vegan diets, too, are becoming more and more popular and again can be such a great way of eating as long as you have a good balance of foods. My daughters are vegan and they have taught me so much. There's loads of good info on the Vegetarian Society and Vegan Society websites so check those out and encourage family members thinking of this way of eating to do the same.

Cooking for older people

It's not just the young ones that can be difficult to feed either. At the other end of the scale, many of us have older relatives to care for or keep an eye on. If you're caring for someone who can't cook any more, that can prove a challenge too. Pippy, my granny and a total legend, lived next door to us for years and I know plenty of people who provide food for elderly neighbours or relatives.

For some older people weight can be an issue as they slow down or perhaps take less exercise because of ill health. Others find their appetite is reduced and they tend not to bother with meals, surviving on snacks and tea and biscuits.

But it is more important than ever to have a good healthy diet as we age. As you get older, the body can be less effective at absorbing nutrients so you need to make sure you have a good balanced diet to keep the digestive system healthy. Dehydration can also be a problem for some elderly people who don't notice they are thirsty and just forget to drink. And with dehydration comes headaches and other symptoms such as constipation and urinary tract infections. UTIs can be devastating to the very elderly.

Quench that thirst

Everyone, regardless of age, needs to remember to drink regularly throughout the day. For the technologically minded there are plenty of apps you can use to jog your memory, or just keep a bottle of water handy or a jugful on your desk. If you're not keen on the taste of your tap water, buy a simple jug filter or add some flavourings such as a slice of orange, a few sliced strawberries, some mint or cucumber – you'll be surprised at the difference this makes.

Fibre why it's so important

I've been hearing more and more about the importance of fibre in our diet recently. I wanted to know more about why and what foods are high in fibre so I talked to my nutritionist. This is what she told me.

Fibre isn't quite as sexy as some other nutrients but it's just as important.

In the latest report from SACN (Scientific Advisory Committee on Nutrition) the recommended fibre intake for adults has been increased from 25g to 30g. The average intake of fibre for men in the UK is around 20g a day and 17g a day for women so most of us have to make a conscious effort to eat more fibre to reach the recommended target. Diets rich in fibre can help protect against heart disease and strokes, type 2 diabetes, bowel cancer, constipation and diverticular disease.

Fibre is found in plant-based foods such as cereals, fruit, vegetables, nuts, beans and pulses. It passes though the digestive tract largely unchanged and undigested but it can be partially digested by bacteria that we all have living in our large intestine. There are two kinds of fibre. Soluble fibre is found in foods such as oats, barley, rye, fruit, root veg, beans, lentils and linseed. It helps to reduce high cholesterol and balance blood sugar. Insoluble fibre, which is found in wholegrain cereals like wholemeal bread, brown rice and fruit and vegetables, helps keep your digestive system moving and your bowels healthy.

The other fantastic thing about fibre is it helps you feel full and satisfied for longer which is a great plus when you're trying to lose weight! And not all high-fibre foods are brown and chewy – for example, avocados, green peas, watermelon and blackberries are all high in fibre. Have a look at these recipes which all contain a good amount of fibre: sweet potato and black bean fritters (page 31), white bean salad (page 50), winter minestrone (page 75), mushroom cobbler (page 145) and blackberry and apple crumble (page 184). See how good fibre can be!

AGE	RECOMMENDED DAILY INTAKE OF FIBRE (APPROX.)
2-5 year olds	15g
5–11 year olds	20g
11–16 year olds	25g
Adults	30g

And here's the fibre content of a selection of foods to give you an idea

FOOD	FIBRE (g)
50g wholemeal pasta (uncooked weight)	6
Bowl of lentil soup	5.5
100g fresh or frozen soya beans	5.4
2 slices of wholemeal bread	5.3
100g wholewheat noodles (uncooked weight)	5.3
2 heaped tbsp (30g) cooked red kidney beans	5
80g peas	4.2
Porridge made with 50g oats	4
50g muesli	4
50g hummus	3.6
50g quinoa (uncooked weight)	3.5
30g almonds	3
100g broccoli	2.8
30g dried apricots	2.5
100g butternut squash (uncooked weight)	2
1 apple	1.8
1 medium banana	1.5
50g brown rice (uncooked weight)	1.5
80g sweetcorn	1.5
2 heaped tbsp (30g) cooked black beans	1.4
100g spinach (uncooked weight)	1

SAMPLE MENU WITH 38g FIBRE	
Breakfast	Porridge and banana: 5.5g fibre
Snack	30g dried apricots: 2.5g fibre
Lunch	Pasta and chickpeas (p.57): 10g fibre
Snack	30g almonds: 3g fibre
Evening meal	Mushroom cobbler (p.145): 12g fibre + Peaches (p.168) 5g fibre

Calories – to count or not to count

Opinions on calorie counting have swung back and forth in recent years. At one time it was THE way to lose weight, then experts started coming up with all sorts of other ideas – eating only certain foods, eating at particular times of day, intermittent fasting and so on. But in the end we've all come round to the realisation that there must be a balance between what goes in and what comes out, between the calories you consume and the energy you use.

I used not to be a fan of calorie counting but now I have realised that it is helpful to keep a check on my intake and I know lots of people find the same. So I've included calorie counts for all the recipes and you will find full nutritional info at the back of the book, noting the carbohydrate, fat, protein, sugar and salt content of each recipe.

So it's up to you. If you or a loved one want to calorie count, you can just eat the recipes in this book that work with your daily calorie allowance and know that you are getting a good, healthy and varied diet.

My 5-week plan

Cooking from the recipes in this book will help to keep you on the straight and narrow – avoiding added and refined sugar and refined carbs and eating plenty of smart carbs, veggies and lean protein.

And if you want to lose weight, have a look at my 5-week plan at the back of the book for menus that will gradually reduce your calorie count and your sugar intake. We've made it easy for you!

A FEW COOKING NOTES

- Peel garlic, onions and other vegetables unless otherwise specified. The weights given in the ingredients lists are the peeled weight.

- Stock is easy and cheap to make and you will find recipes for a vegetable stock and a chicken stock on pages 198 and 199 of this book. But if you run out or don't have time, use the good ready-made fresh stocks you can buy in supermarkets now. Heat the stock first before adding it to your other ingredients – saves lots of time.

- I like to use free-range chicken and eggs whenever I can, but that's your call.

- I've flagged up vegetarian (V) and vegan (Ve) recipes and noted where others can be made vegetarian by leaving out certain ingredients. Where cheese is included in a vegetarian recipe, be aware that some cheeses like Parmesan are not suitable for vegetarians but there are plenty of vegetarian alternatives available in supermarkets now.

We eat a lot of eggs in our house. They are yummy as well as full of the goodness, minerals and protein that we all need to stay strong and healthy and stave off snacking later in the morning. In fact, I'd go as far as to say that eggs are the best breakfast food ever, ever as far as I'm concerned. I totally love them. I've read recently that people who eat eggs for breakfast go on to consume *fewer calories* during the rest of the day. So that has to be good! Obviously simple egg dishes such as omelettes are perfect, but I've included some of my other faves here which you might like to try for a weekend brunch, such as French toast and delish huevos rancheros. When you don't feel like eggs or if you are vegan, try my tacos – they are amaaaaaaazing! (My daughters have gone vegan so there are lots of vegan comments in this book.)

Breakfast and Brunch

Savoury French Toast

I've always loved French toast but I tend to avoid the sweet version with maple syrup these days. So I'm thrilled to share this savoury variation which is unbelievably yum. A great Sunday brunch.

Serves 4

3 large eggs

300ml whole milk

50g vegetarian Parmesan-style cheese, grated

1 tsp dried or fresh tarragon leaves

1 garlic clove (optional)

4 thick slices of wholemeal bread, cut in half if large

15g butter

4 branches of cherry vine tomatoes

To serve

4 tbsp ricotta

a few chives, finely chopped

1. Break the eggs into a bowl and add the milk, grated cheese and tarragon. Season them well with salt and pepper, then whisk until well combined. If you're using the garlic, cut the clove in half and rub the cut side over the slices of bread.

2. Heat a teaspoon of olive oil with the butter in a large frying pan. Dip each slice of bread into the egg and milk mixture until completely soaked through. Wipe off any excess and add the slices to the frying pan. Cook the slices of bread on each side for 3–4 minutes until they're crisp and well browned, then drain them on kitchen paper.

3. Meanwhile, heat another teaspoon of oil in a small frying pan and add the tomatoes. Cook the tomatoes for several minutes, shaking the pan regularly, until they have puffed up and are just cooked through. Season them with salt and pepper.

4. Serve the French toast with the tomatoes, ricotta and chopped chives.

Oat Pancakes with Apple Compote

I'm loving these oaty pancakes. Just remember to make the batter at the last minute – if you leave it hanging around too long, the milk will quickly be absorbed by the oats and the batter will get too thick. You could try different fruit compotes but I think this apple one is just right. Softer eating apples, such as Coxes, are best here – not crisp Granny Smiths.

Serves 4

200g porridge oats
2 tsp baking powder
1 tsp ground cinnamon
grating of nutmeg
2 eggs
250ml milk or oat milk

Compote

4 eating apples, peeled,
   cored and diced
1 tsp cinnamon
25g butter

1. For the compote, put the apples in a saucepan with the cinnamon and butter. Add 2–3 tablespoons of water and cover the pan. Cook gently until the apples have softened, then take the lid off the pan and leave the compote to simmer and thicken slightly. You could add a drizzle of maple syrup if you like but the fruit shouldn't need it.

2. Meanwhile, for the pancakes, put 150g of the oats into a food processor or blender and blitz to the texture of wholemeal flour. Add the rest of the porridge oats and give them a quick whizz to break them up too – you should end up with a nice mixture of textures. Tip the oats into a bowl and add the baking powder, spices and a generous pinch of salt.

3. Whisk the eggs into the milk, then pour the mixture into the dry ingredients. Stir to make a batter – the consistency shouldn't be too thick and you should just still be able to pour the mixture.

4. Add a little oil (or butter) to a large frying pan. Dollop a few spoonfuls of the batter on to the frying pan. When the pancakes have set on the underside and have turned a deep golden brown, flip them over and cook for a further couple of minutes. Remove them from the pan and keep them warm.

5. Continue until you have used up all the batter – you should be able to make 16 pancakes. If you find the batter starts to thicken up too much, thin it with a little more milk.

6. Serve the pancakes immediately with the compote and some yoghurt or crème fraiche if you like.

Classic French Omelette

I'm half French so making the perfect omelette is in my DNA! You can do all sorts of clever stuff with omelettes, but really I think the classic French version with finely chopped herbs is probably the best of all. Simple, chic and satisfying.

Serves 1

3 eggs
1 tbsp each of finely
  chopped parsley,
  chives and tarragon
5g butter

1. Crack the eggs into a bowl and season them with salt and pepper. Break up the yolks and combine them with the whites. Don't beat the eggs too much – you don't want to work a lot of air into the mixture. Reserve a little of each of the herbs to garnish the finished omelette and stir the rest into the eggs.

2. Melt the butter in a frying or omelette pan over a medium heat. Add the eggs and swirl them around so the whole base of the pan is covered. Leave them for a few moments so the underside sets, then, using a fork, pull the edges into the centre of the pan, letting the runny egg fill the gaps. Continue to do this until the omelette is almost completely set.

3. For an omelette with a soft, moussy interior, fold the sides into the centre at this point. Roll the omelette over on to a plate so the underside is facing upwards and the join is on the bottom. If you want a completely set omelette, leave it in the pan for a little longer before folding and rolling, then continue in the same way. The underside will have taken on more colour.

4. Sprinkle with the remaining herbs and enjoy immediately.

Rolled Omelette

It's good to make this omelette in a fairly large pan so it's nice and thin and easy to roll up. Obviously you can vary the fillings as you like, but this spinach and salmon version is my favourite. It's really healthy, beautifully easy and quick to make and sooooo delish.

Serves 2

150g baby leaf spinach
10g butter
3 eggs
100g hot smoked
  salmon, flaked
squeeze of lemon juice

1. Wash the spinach thoroughly – don't bother about shaking off too much of the water. Put the spinach into a saucepan, season with salt and pepper and heat it gently until it has all wilted down. Tip the spinach into a sieve or colander and leave it to drain.

2. Meanwhile, melt the butter in a large frying pan. Gently beat the eggs in a bowl and season them with salt and pepper. When the butter is foaming, add the beaten eggs and swirl them around the pan until they completely cover the base in an even layer. As the edges cook, push them into the centre and allow the gaps to fill with uncooked egg, until the whole omelette is almost set – it should be fairly thin. How much you cook it is up to you, but I like to have a hint of moisture in the middle.

3. Sprinkle the spinach and salmon on top of the omelette and squeeze over some lemon juice. Transfer the omelette to a board and roll it up fairly tightly. Cut it into slices and serve at once.

Baked Eggs with Chorizo and Red Peppers

As everyone probably knows by now, I completely LOVE eggs. This makes an amaaaazing brunch or lunch dish – loads of flavour and super easy to put together.

Serves 4

100g cooking chorizo, diced

1 red onion, sliced into wedges

2 red peppers, deseeded and thickly sliced

400g can of chopped tomatoes

½ tsp hot paprika

1 tsp oregano

150g spinach, well washed

4 eggs

2 tbsp finely chopped parsley, to garnish

To serve (optional)

toast, Greek yoghurt

1. Preheat the oven to 200°C/Fan 180°C/Gas 6. Add a teaspoon of olive oil to an ovenproof frying pan and pile in the chorizo, onion wedges and red peppers.

2. Cook for several minutes until the onions and peppers have started to soften, then add the tomatoes, paprika and oregano. Simmer for 10 minutes until the sauce has reduced a little. Pile the spinach on top and leave it for a few seconds to wilt down, then stir it into the sauce.

3. Make 4 shallow indentations in the sauce with a spoon, then carefully crack an egg into each one.

4. Put the pan in the oven and bake for 10 minutes, until the whites of the eggs are set, but the yolks are still runny. Remove the pan from the oven and sprinkle over some parsley.

5. Serve with toast and perhaps some yoghurt on the side if you like.

   DAVINA'S TIP: *If you're cutting back on meat or you prefer a vegetarian brunch, leave out the chorizo and add some extra smoked paprika to taste.*

Huevos Rancheros

This Mexican breakfast is one of my family's favourite weekend treats. You can get the refried beans ready the day before if you like, then whip the whole thing up in minutes when you're ready for brunch. And yes, there are more than ten ingredients but there are really two recipes here and you can also use the refried beans for my fab tacos on page 32. Chipotle (chi-pot-leh – I used to say chi-pottle!) paste is made from tomatoes, onion, chillies and spices and it features in many Mexican dishes. You can buy it in supermarkets.

Serves 4

4 corn tortillas
(bought or see p.197)

4 eggs

Refried beans

2 red onions, coarsely diced

1 red pepper, diced

2 garlic cloves, crushed

1 tsp oregano

1 tsp ground cumin

1 tsp–1 tbsp chipotle paste
(to taste)

400g can of pinto or black
beans, drained

To garnish

coriander leaves

4 tbsp soured cream

lime wedges

1 portion of raw tomato
salsa – see p.193 (optional)

50g vegetarian Cheddar or
similar hard cheese,
grated (optional)

1. First make the refried beans. Heat a tablespoon of oil in a large frying pan and add the onions and pepper. Cook them over a medium heat, stirring regularly, until they're softened and browning slightly around the edges, then add the garlic, oregano, cumin, chipotle paste and beans.

2. Pour in 200ml of water, then season with salt and pepper. Bring the mixture to the boil, then turn down the heat and simmer until the onions and pepper are soft and most of the liquid is absorbed. Mash briefly to break up some of the beans, then continue to cook for a few more minutes, stirring constantly.

3. Assemble all the garnishes and put them on the table. Warm the tortillas in a dry frying pan over a medium heat, then wrap them in a tea towel to keep them warm. Heat a tablespoon of olive oil or butter in a frying pan and cook the eggs to your liking.

4. Serve the eggs with the refried beans and warm tortillas and as many of the garnishes as you like.

DAVINA'S TIP: *Beans are a good source of fibre as well as protein so are really good for you as well as nice to eat.*

Sweet Potato and Black Bean Fritters

It's really worth making the mixture for these yummy little fritters the night before you want to cook them. It improves the texture and think how nice it is to get up knowing that these are for breakfast – mmmmmm. If you're vegan you can still enjoy them – just use an egg substitute for binding. You'll find a range of different types in the shops.

Serves 4

1 large sweet potato, diced (about 500g peeled weight)

1 onion, finely chopped

2 garlic cloves, finely chopped

zest of 2 limes

small bunch of coriander, finely chopped

400g can of black beans, drained

50g wholemeal plain flour

1 egg

To serve

lime wedges and hot sauce

1. Bring a saucepan of water to the boil and add salt. Add the sweet potato and cook for about 10 minutes until it's just tender. Drain it into a colander and leave it to cool down and dry out a little.

2. Heat a tablespoon of olive oil in a frying pan. Add the onion and cook it gently until very soft and translucent. Add the garlic and continue to cook for 2–3 more minutes, then remove the pan from the heat and leave the onion and garlic to cool.

3. Put the sweet potato in a bowl and mash it roughly. Add the cooled onion and garlic, then all the remaining ingredients, except the lime and hot sauce. Season generously, then stir everything together, making sure it is completely combined. The mixture will be fairly soft and sticky so leave it to chill for a while if you have time to make it easier to handle.

4. Divide the mixture into 8 flat fritters, about 11–12cm in diameter. Heat some olive oil in a large, preferably non-stick, frying pan and fry a few of the fritters for 4–5 minutes on each side until they're crisp and brown. Don't overcrowd the pan – the fritters will be fragile and you need space around them for manoeuvring. Keep the first batch warm while you cook the rest.

5. Serve the fritters with lime wedges to squeeze over them and some hot sauce on the side for those who fancy it.

Tacos

This makes such a fun weekend brunch. You can buy tortillas in most supermarkets now and once everything is ready, just put it all on the table and let everyone make their own Mexican feast. Timings above are if you've made the beans in advance – this will take a bit longer if not. Adding broccoli and mushrooms isn't traditional but it's a good way of upping your five a day.

Serves 4

8 corn tortillas

Avocado crema
juice of 1 lime
2 avocados, peeled
and pitted

Filling
2 garlic cloves, finely
sliced
2 chillies, deseeded and
thinly sliced
400g sprouting broccoli,
cut into short lengths
400g chestnut
mushrooms, cut
into quarters

To garnish
1 quantity of refried
beans (see p.28)
a few coriander leaves
100g vegetarian Cheddar
cheese, grated (optional)

1. To make the avocado crema, put the lime juice into a bowl with a large pinch of sea salt. Add the avocado flesh and mash until smooth. Taste for seasoning and add more salt or lime juice if necessary.

2. To prepare the filling, heat a tablespoon of olive oil in a wok or frying pan. Add the garlic and chillies and fry for a minute. Add the sprouting broccoli and continue to stir-fry for another 2 minutes, then add the mushrooms. Season with salt and pepper. Continue to fry for 2–3 minutes, then remove the pan from the heat.

3. Heat a heavy-based frying pan or griddle until very hot. Warm the tortillas for about 10 seconds on each side, then wrap them in a tea towel on a plate or in a basket to bring to the table.

4. To assemble, spread a spoonful of refried beans in the centre of a tortilla. Top with some broccoli and mushrooms, followed by avocado crema and garnishes.

DAVINA'S TIP: *I've suggested using bought tortillas here for speed, but it's really easy to make your own if you feel like it (see p.197). Try it and see – it's fun for the children too.*

 (leave out cheese)

Stuffed Eggs

I never tire of eggs and these little stuffed goodies make a nice dish for brunch or any time of day. Light and tasty – I hope you're going to love, love, love them. Kids like making these too.

Serves 2–4

4 eggs

Spinach filling (for 2 eggs)

50g frozen spinach, defrosted

30g cream cheese – a goat's one is good for flavour

¼ tsp mustard powder

1 tbsp lemon juice

Prawn filling (for 2 eggs)

50g North Atlantic shelled prawns or brown shrimp, plus 4 extra to garnish

25g cream cheese

½ tsp tomato purée

1 tbsp lemon juice

To serve

smoked paprika and some cress

 (spinach version)

1. The night before making this, if you remember, lie the eggs on their sides rather than with points facing upwards. This will help centre the yolk when boiled.

2. Put the eggs in a saucepan and cover them with water. Bring the water to the boil, then turn the heat down and leave the eggs to simmer gently for 10 minutes. Remove the eggs and run them under cold water until completely cold. Peel the eggs and cut them in half lengthways. Carefully take out the yolks and divide them between 2 bowls.

3. To make the spinach filling, squeeze out as much water from the spinach as you can. Put it in a small food processor with the cream cheese, mustard powder, 2 of the egg yolks and the lemon juice. Season generously with salt and pepper, then blitz until smooth – you may need to push the mixture down the sides a couple of times.

4. To make the prawn filling, put the prawns or shrimp in a small food processor with the cream cheese, the remaining 2 egg yolks, tomato purée and lemon juice. Proceed as above.

5. To fill the eggs, spoon the fillings into the cavities left by the yolks. Don't worry if it spills over the edges a little. Alternatively, put the fillings into piping bags and pipe them in.

6. Garnish with a sprinkling of paprika and cress. Top each of the prawn-filled eggs with a prawn.

Apple Soda Bread

This is so good just as it is or you can serve it with butter and honey or wedges of cheese if you like. Great toasted too and it freezes well. I like to freeze slices that I can whip out and pop into the toaster when someone fancies a snack. Malt extract, by the way, is lovely syrupy stuff that you can use in small quantities in baking instead of refined sugar. And I've realised that there's nothing weird about buttermilk – you'll find it in most supermarkets. Spelt flour is great but you can also use wholemeal – which is cheaper. ♡

Makes 12 slices

500g wholemeal flour
(wheat or spelt)
1 tsp bicarbonate of soda
1 tbsp malt extract
400ml buttermilk
1 eating apple, peeled
and finely chopped
50g raisins

1. Preheat the oven to 200°C/Fan 180°C/Gas 6.

2. Mix the flour, bicarbonate of soda and a teaspoon of salt in a large bowl. Whisk the malt extract and buttermilk together in a jug until well combined and the mixture is a light honey colour.

3. Pat the pieces of apple dry with kitchen paper and add them to the dry ingredients along with the raisins. Make a well in the centre and pour in the malt extract and buttermilk. Mix thoroughly, as quickly and as firmly as you can. The mixture will be quite sticky.

4. Pile the mixture on to the centre of a baking tray and shape it into a round about 22cm in diameter. Smooth it over with a palette knife (it's easiest to work up from the sides to the top and centre) and gently press down any raisins or pieces of apple poking through so they don't burn when the bread is in the oven. Score a cross on the top of the dough.

5. Bake the bread in the oven for 30–35 minutes until it is well risen and the crust is a rich golden brown. It should sound hollow when tapped on the underside. Delicious hot from the oven or when cooled.

I love it when as many people in the house as possible all sit down to eat together. But life gets in the way of the best-laid plans and our weekdays can be busy with work and school. Lunch has to be a moveable feast. The recipes in this chapter are super delish whether eaten at home or piled into some Tupperware to take out with you. And they're great for picnics or family outings, way better than soggy sandwiches and cheaper too. They are also easily portable to cook for someone else and take to their kitchen. Try the sweetcorn and asparagus soup with a pesto and mozzarella roll on the side. Or pack up some falafel Scotch eggs with a serving of celeriac and lentil salad – YUM and such a refreshing change from the usual. The calzone pizzas are ridiculously good and make a perfect eat-in-your-hand feast to take along on a day out.

Lunch on the Run

Sweetcorn and Asparagus Soup

A steaming bowl of soup is my perfect lunch and this recipe is one of my faves. It's quick to make, and ideal for taking to work for lunch at your desk. Just pack the garnishes in a separate box and add them when you're ready. And if you use veg stock and leave out the chicken, this makes a good vegetarian or vegan dish. Just check that your soy sauce is vegan-friendly – most are.

Serves 4

500g sweetcorn (frozen is fine)

bunch of spring onions, cut into rounds

30g fresh root ginger, finely chopped

1 litre hot chicken or vegetable stock

2 tbsp light soy sauce

To garnish

200g cooked chicken, shredded (optional)

small bunch of mint, leaves only

1 tsp sesame oil

lime wedges

1. Put about one-third of the sweetcorn in a food processor and give it a quick blitz to break it up. You don't want it to be smooth, but just broken down enough to give texture to the soup and thicken it slightly. Tip it into a saucepan, then add the rest of the sweetcorn with half the spring onions and the root ginger.

2. Pour over the hot stock and add the soy sauce. Bring the soup to the boil, then turn the heat down and leave it to simmer for 10 minutes to allow the flavours to combine. Taste for seasoning and add salt and pepper.

3. Add the asparagus tips and simmer for another 2–3 minutes. Add the cooked chicken, if using, and the rest of the spring onions. Serve garnished with the mint leaves, the sesame oil and some lime wedges for squeezing over the soup.

Pesto and Mozzarella Rolls

These tear-and-share type rolls are such fun and just right with a bowl of soup for lunch. They freeze really well so you can whip one out of the freezer, wrap it in foil and reheat it in a medium oven (about 160°C/Fan 140°C/Gas 3) for 15–20 minutes. The type of mozzarella you buy in blocks works best for this recipe as it contains less moisture – you don't want soggy dough.

Makes 12 rolls

500g wholemeal flour or malted wholegrain flour, plus extra for dusting

7g dried instant yeast

Filling

1 quantity of green or red pesto, or ½ quantities of each (see p.192)

250g block of mozzarella, coarsely grated

beaten egg, for brushing

1. Mix the flour and yeast in a large bowl, and sprinkle over a teaspoon of salt. Drizzle in 2 tablespoons of olive oil, then gradually work in about 300ml of tepid water to make a fairly soft, sticky dough. You may need more or less water. Turn the bread dough out on to a floured surface and knead it for about 10 minutes until the dough is very smooth and elastic.

2. Put the dough into a lightly oiled bowl and cover it with cling film or a damp tea towel. Leave it somewhere warm to prove and double in size. This will take 1–3 hours. When the dough is well risen, knock it back to get rid of some of the air, then turn it out again on to a floured work surface. Roll and shape it into a rectangle about 40 x 30cm. It will take a while before the dough stops springing back, but persevere.

3. Spread the pesto over the dough – if you want to use both types, cover one half with the green and the other half with the red. Keep back about 50g of the mozzarella and sprinkle the rest over the pesto. Roll up the dough from one of the longer sides into a sausage shape.

4. Cut the dough into 12 evenly sized rolls. Line a baking tin with baking paper and arrange the rolls swirl-side up, tucking the outside end of the rolls under slightly. Cover the rolls with cling film or a damp tea towel and leave them to prove for another 30 minutes or so until well risen and springy again. Preheat the oven to 200°C/Fan 180°C/Gas 6.

5. Brush the dough with beaten egg and sprinkle over the remaining grated mozzarella. Bake the rolls in the preheated oven for 30–35 minutes. Lift the rolls all together, still on their baking paper, off the tin and transfer them to a wire rack to cool.

Calzone

A calzone is a filled pizza and great to take along on a day out. The whole ones make a hearty meal or you could make eight half-sized versions for a smaller snack. One tip – the blocks of mozzarella work better than the balls for this recipe, but if you can only find the balls, drain them well before using.

Makes 4

250g strong wholemeal flour, plus extra for dusting

1 tsp instant yeast

200g mushrooms, quartered

1 garlic clove, finely chopped

2 roasted red peppers, cut into strips (from a jar or see p.196)

200g cherry tomatoes, quartered

small bunch of basil

25g vegetarian Parmesan-style cheese, grated

block of mozzarella (250g), sliced

1. To make the dough, put the flour and yeast in a bowl and add half a teaspoon of salt. Mix to combine, then gradually work in 150ml of warm water and 25ml of olive oil. When you have a rough dough, turn it out on to a work surface and knead until it is smooth and pliable. Put the dough in a bowl and cover it with a damp cloth or cling film. Leave it to prove for at least an hour until it has doubled in size.

2. Next prepare the filling. Heat a tablespoon of olive oil in a frying pan. Add the mushrooms with a pinch of salt and fry them until well browned. Add the garlic and cook for a further couple of minutes. Remove the pan from the heat and leave the mushrooms to cool down.

3. Preheat your oven to its highest setting.

4. Cut the dough into 4 pieces and roll each one out into a thin round. Arrange a quarter of the mushrooms over one half of the first round of dough, then top with a quarter of the peppers, tomatoes and basil. Sprinkle with Parmesan, season well and lay over a quarter of the slices of mozzarella. Pull the uncovered side of dough over the filling, then crimp the edges together – the traditional way to do it is to roll them upwards. Cut a couple of slits in the middle of the calzone. Repeat to make the rest.

5. Lightly flour a baking tray and place the calzones on top. Bake them in the oven for 12–15 minutes until they are well-risen and golden brown. Allow them to cool a little before eating – they'll be volcanic inside! If you're taking them out for a picnic or a packed lunch, wrap them in some baking paper and foil.

Nutty Noodle Salad

Do you remember all the excitement a few years ago when some scientists announced that cold or reheated pasta is actually better for you than freshly cooked? It causes less of a surge in blood sugar apparently. This dish makes good use of this discovery and tastes yummy too – I do love peanut butter dressing. Leftover roast chicken is ideal for this or you can buy some cooked chicken or grill a breast or thigh.

Serves 4

4 nests of wholemeal egg noodles

1 tsp sesame oil

200g cooked chicken, shredded

4 spring onions, finely sliced

100g mangetout, finely sliced lengthways on the diagonal

100g baby corn, finely sliced lengthways on the diagonal

Dressing

75g peanut butter (crunchy or smooth)

2 tbsp soy sauce

juice of 1 lime

1 garlic clove, finely chopped

1. Cook the noodles according to the packet instructions, then run them under cold water to cool them quickly. Toss them in the sesame oil and put them in a bowl with the other salad ingredients.

2. To make the dressing, mix the peanut butter, soy sauce, lime juice and garlic in a small jug – you could add a teaspoon of hot sauce too if you like things spicy. Whisk everything together, adding up to 3 tablespoons of warm water to get a mixture with the consistency of single cream. Add salt and pepper to taste.

3. Pour the dressing over the noodles and toss to combine. Divide the salad between 4 bowls or use portable containers if you're having this as a packed lunch. Sprinkle with some chopped mint or coriander if you like.

Falafel Scotch Eggs

These are the perfect food for a family picnic – easy to transport and good to eat with your fingers.
I've always liked Scotch eggs and it's great to have a veggie version with this falafel-style coating.
I know deep-frying is a bit naughty but once in a while… as Pippy (my granny) says,
'A little of what you fancy does you good'. Lovely with the mint and yoghurt sauce on page 193.

Makes 6

7 eggs
1 onion, very finely
    chopped
2 garlic cloves, finely
    chopped
1 tsp ground cumin
small bunch of parsley,
    finely chopped
zest of 1 lemon
400g can of chickpeas,
    drained
75g wholemeal
    breadcrumbs
50g plain flour

1. Bring a pan of water to the boil and gently lower in 6 of the eggs. Boil for 6 minutes, then drain and run the eggs under cold water until cool.

2. Heat a tablespoon of olive oil in a frying pan and add the onion. Gently fry the onion until it's very soft, then add the garlic and cumin. Stir for another couple of minutes, then remove from the heat and leave to cool.

3. Put the onion mixture in a food processor with the parsley, lemon zest and chickpeas, then season well with salt and pepper. Pulse until you have a paste with some texture to it – the mixture should stick together without crumbling. Stir in 25g of the breadcrumbs and mix thoroughly. Tip everything into a bowl and chill well for at least an hour.

4. Peel the eggs and rinse them if any bits of shell remain. Pat them dry and dust them with the flour. Beat the remaining egg in a shallow bowl and put the rest of the breadcrumbs in another bowl.

5. Divide the chickpea mixture into 6 equal pieces. Dust your hands with flour, flatten a piece in your hands, then mould it round an egg, making sure the covering is as even as possible. Dip it into the beaten egg, then roll it in the breadcrumbs to coat it completely. Repeat with the remaining eggs, then chill them for another hour or so if you have time.

6. To cook, half-fill a deep saucepan or a deep-fat fryer with vegetable oil and heat it to 160°C. If you don't have a thermometer, drop in a cube of bread – it should turn a light golden-brown in 30 seconds. Cook the eggs, a few at a time, for about 8 minutes until the coating is a deep golden brown. Drain the eggs on kitchen paper and serve them hot or cold.

White Bean Salad

This is filling, nourishing, full of fibre and protein – the ideal lunch on a busy day. Love it. Canned beans are fine but you could also cook up a big batch of dried beans when you have time and keep them in the freezer for making quick salads like this one. You'll find sunblush tomatoes in the supermarket, either on the deli counter or in little tubs. Yum, yum, yum.

Serves 4

1 red onion, very finely sliced

100g rocket leaves, roughly chopped

2 x 400g cans of cannellini beans, drained

50g black olives, pitted

25g capers, rinsed

160g can of tuna in spring water

50g sunblush tomatoes, roughly chopped

1 garlic clove, crushed

1 tsp balsamic vinegar

a few basil and parsley leaves, to garnish

1. Soak the onion slices in iced water for 10 minutes, then drain them – this removes any bitterness.

2. Put the rocket, beans, olives and capers in a bowl. Drain the water from the can of tuna into a separate bowl, then flake the tuna into the beans. Add the drained onion slices and half the sunblush tomatoes.

3. Put the remaining tomatoes in a food processor with a tablespoon of olive oil (some of the oil from the sunblush tomatoes is fine), the garlic, balsamic vinegar and a tablespoon of the water from the tuna. Blitz to make a dressing, adding a little more water if it's too thick, then drizzle this over the salad ingredients. Stir to combine and garnish with the basil and parsley leaves.

4. If you're taking this salad as a packed lunch, take the dressing in a separate pot and add it just before eating.

DAVINA'S TIP: *This is a great high-fibre recipe – one serving gives you a third of your recommended daily intake.*

Roast Squash Salad with Feta

I often cook squash and particularly love it roasted as it has a lovely sweet flavour. Don't throw away the seeds – wash and dry them carefully, then fry them and they make a lovely snack or garnish. Why pay good money for a pack of pumpkin seeds when they're there for the taking? Harissa is that spicy paste from North Africa and it's available in jars in supermarkets.

Serves 4

500g squash, cut into
   chunks, seeds reserved

harissa paste

2 red onions, cut into thin
   wedges

leaves from a large sprig
   of thyme

200g feta cheese, cut
   into chunks

100g giant couscous

juice of 1 lemon

1 tsp honey (optional)

150g baby salad leaves

a few mint or parsley
   leaves, to garnish

1. Preheat the oven to 200°C/Fan 180°C/Gas 6. Put the squash in a bowl and add 2 tablespoons of harissa paste, rubbing it into the squash flesh. Arrange the squash in a roasting tin with the wedges of onion and season with salt and pepper. Sprinkle with the thyme leaves and drizzle over 2 tablespoons of olive oil.

2. Roast the squash and onions for 25 minutes, then brush the feta chunks with a teaspoon of olive oil and add them to the vegetables. Roast for a further 10 minutes, until the feta is slightly puffed up and starting to colour, then remove the tin from the oven.

3. Wash the squash seeds thoroughly to get rid of any orange tendrils, then dry them with kitchen paper. Put the seeds in a frying pan with a tablespoon of oil and fry them until lightly coloured. Keep stirring or shaking the pan regularly. Season the seeds with salt and leave to cool.

4. Meanwhile, cook the giant couscous. Bring a saucepan of water to the boil and add plenty of salt. Add the couscous and cook for 8 minutes or until cooked, then drain.

5. For the dressing, whisk 2 tablespoons of olive oil with the lemon juice, honey, if using, and a teaspoon of harissa. Season with salt and pepper.

6. To assemble, add a tablespoon of the dressing to the couscous and mix thoroughly. Arrange the salad in a bowl or lunchboxes, toss with the salad leaves and top with the squash and feta. When you're ready to eat, drizzle over the remaining dressing and garnish with the herbs and some toasted squash seeds.

Freekeh and Goat's Cheese Salad

I'd never heard of freekeh until I started doing my cookbooks and met some knowledgeable foodies! Now I'm a fan and I find it makes a great salad. Freekeh is a grain that comes from young durum wheat that's roasted and then cracked. It has a good smoky flavour and contains plenty of protein, fibre and vitamins. It's the perfect partner for some creamy goat's cheese too.

Serves 4

1 red onion, finely sliced
100g freekeh
zest and juice of ½ lemon
juice of 1 orange
½ tsp cinnamon
150g salad leaves
1 carrot, peeled and cut
  into matchsticks
6 fat, soft Medjool dates,
  pitted and thinly sliced
50g goat's cream cheese
small bunch of mint,
  coriander or parsley
  leaves, to garnish, or a
  mixture of all 3

1. Put the onion slices in a bowl of iced water and leave them to soak for 10 minutes, then drain. Rinse the freekeh thoroughly and soak it in cold water for 5 minutes.

2. Drain the freekeh thoroughly, then put it in a saucepan and cover with 300ml of water (or you can use vegetable stock for extra flavour). Season with salt and pepper. Bring to the boil, then turn down the heat and cover the pan. Simmer the freekeh for up to 20 minutes, checking after 15 minutes, until it is cooked through and the liquid has been absorbed. Set it aside to cool.

3. Whisk 2 tablespoons of olive oil with the lemon zest and juice, orange juice and cinnamon in a small jug. Season with salt and pepper.

4. To assemble, put the freekeh in a bowl (or in a plastic box for lunch on the go) and drizzle over half the dressing. Top with the leaves, carrot and drained onion slices, then arrange the dates over the top. Spoon teaspoons of the goat's cheese over the salad. When you're ready to eat, add the remaining salad dressing and garnish with plenty of herbs. If you're serving this one at home it looks lovely on a big platter.

Pasta and Chickpeas

On a chilly day it's nice to have something hot for lunch whether you're at home or work. Pile this pasta dish into a Thermos flask and you will be so happy come lunchtime. It's an adaptation of an Italian classic but with added veg for goodness and fibre. And if you leave the bacon out and use vegetarian cheese, this could be a good veggie meal.

Serves 4

200g wholewheat pasta
200g baby leaf spinach
100g diced bacon
2 garlic cloves, finely
   chopped
2 fresh tomatoes, peeled
   and diced
1 sprig of rosemary,
   chopped
400g can of chickpeas,
   drained
grated Parmesan
   cheese (or vegetarian
   equivalent), to serve

1. Bring a large saucepan of water to the boil. Add plenty of salt, then the pasta. Cook the pasta for 10–12 minutes until just al dente, then add the spinach and allow it to wilt down into the water before draining everything in a colander.

2. While the pasta is cooking, heat 2 tablespoons of olive oil in a large saucepan or in a sauté pan with a lid. Add the bacon and fry it until crisp and browned. Add the garlic and cook for a further minute or so, then add the tomatoes and rosemary along with 100ml of water. Season with salt and pepper, then simmer until reduced.

3. Mash half the chickpeas roughly (you can do this in a food processor or with a hand-held blender) and add them to the sauce with the whole chickpeas. Add a little more water to loosen the sauce and simmer until everything is well combined and piping hot.

4. Toss the sauce with drained pasta and spinach and serve with plenty of grated cheese.

Quinoa and Chorizo Salad

Quinoa is a regular in our house now and all the family enjoy it. You can buy it ready-cooked in packets but it's no trouble to do it yourself, honest, and it's much cheaper. I like to cook extra while I'm about it and stash some in the fridge for another time – yum, yum.

Serves 4

75g quinoa

250g frozen sweetcorn kernels, defrosted

100g cooking chorizo, thinly sliced into rounds

juice of 1 lime

1 garlic clove, crushed

1 tsp ground cumin

½ tsp smoked paprika (hot or sweet, to taste)

200g salad leaves

200g cherry tomatoes, halved

a few coriander leaves, to serve

1. Rinse the quinoa thoroughly – and if you have time, leave it to soak in a bowl of cold water for 5 minutes. Drain it thoroughly, then put it in a small saucepan. Dry fry and stir until all the moisture has evaporated off and the quinoa starts to smell nutty, then cover it with 150ml of water and season with salt and pepper. Bring it to the boil, then turn down the heat and cover the pan. Cook for about 15 minutes until all the liquid has been absorbed and the quinoa has unfurled. Remove the pan from the heat and leave the quinoa to stand, covered, until you need it.

2. Heat a tablespoon of olive oil in a frying pan. Add the sweetcorn kernels and fry them over a medium to high heat until they're lightly charred all over. Remove the pan from the heat, tip the sweetcorn into a bowl and leave it to cool.

3. Add the chorizo to the same pan – no need to add more oil – and fry it on both sides until plenty of fat has rendered out and the rounds are crisp and slightly charred. Drain them on kitchen paper.

4. For the dressing, whisk a tablespoon of olive oil with the lime juice, garlic, cumin and smoked paprika and season with salt and pepper.

5. To assemble the salad, arrange the salad leaves and quinoa on a large serving platter – or in boxes if taking the salad to work. Top with the sweetcorn, chorizo and cherry tomatoes. When you're ready to eat, drizzle over the dressing and add a sprinkling of coriander leaves.

    DAVINA'S TIP: *For a veggie option, leave out the chorizo and add some strips of roasted red peppers (from a jar or see p.196) instead.*

Celeriac and Lentil Salad

A tasty vegan dish – I'm learning just how delish vegan food can be and this salad is a goody.
If you fancy, you could add some matchsticks of carrot too. Perfect for a packed lunch.

Serves 4

½ celeriac, peeled and cut
    into matchsticks
1 crisp eating apple, cut
    into matchsticks
squeeze of lemon juice
200g cooked puy lentils
150g frisée leaves
    or similar
1 tbsp hazelnuts
1 tbsp red wine or
    sherry vinegar
1 tsp mustard
½ tsp maple syrup

1. Put the celeriac and apple in a bowl and season them with salt and pepper. Squeeze over the lemon juice and toss everything together so the apple doesn't go brown.

2. Add the lentils and salad leaves. Toast the hazelnuts in a dry frying pan for a few moments until they've turned golden, then crush them lightly and add them to the salad.

3. Whisk the vinegar, mustard and maple syrup with 2 tablespoons of olive oil in a small jug and season with salt and pepper. Add a little water to the dressing if it is very thick. Dress the salad just before serving.

DAVINA'S TIP: *You can buy ready-cooked puy lentils which are very handy, but it's cheaper to cook them yourself. Rinse 100g of dried lentils, then put them in a pan and cover with cold water. Bring to the boil and simmer them for about 25 minutes until cooked but still with a bit of bite to them. Drain the lentils, then refresh under cold running water.*

Pea and Ricotta Dip

A dip is a great thing to have in the fridge for when hunger pangs strike and this also makes a good snack to take to work or school. Just pack the dip in a box and take a bag of raw veg or crackers along too. At home, this can also make a nice starter, served on rounds of toasted sourdough.

Serves 4

250g fresh or frozen peas, defrosted if frozen

50g ricotta

25g vegetarian Parmesan-style cheese, grated

1 tsp dried mint

zest and juice of ½ lemon

To serve

raw veg (carrot sticks, radishes, cucumber)

rounds of sourdough, toasted

1 garlic clove, halved

grated vegetarian Parmesan-style cheese

1. Bring a saucepan of water to the boil and add salt. Add the peas and blanch them for 2 minutes, then drain them and leave to cool. You can speed the cooling up if you like by running the peas under cold water.

2. Put two-thirds of the peas in a food processor with the ricotta, grated cheese, mint, lemon zest and juice and 2 tablespoons of olive oil. Process in short, sharp bursts, using the pulse button, until you have a rough paste – you don't want the dip to be too smooth. Season with salt and pepper and pulse again, then stir in the reserved peas. The dip should have a nice chunky texture.

3. Enjoy with a pile of raw veg sticks or pile the dip on top of crackers or rounds of toast. If serving with toast, rub the toast with a cut clove of garlic before spreading it with the dip and then sprinkle on a little more grated cheese.

Chicken on Little Gems

This is old-school coronation chicken – which I love – meets the super-cool Thai dish known as laab. Basically it's a sweet/salty/hot/sour chicken and mango mixture, which you serve spooned on to lettuce leaves – so doing away with high-cal crackers or bread. I love that this is so tasty yet really low in calories.

Serves 4

2 cooked chicken
    breasts, diced

1 mango, peeled and
    finely diced

4 spring onions,
    finely sliced

1 tbsp soy or fish sauce

juice and zest of ½ lime

½ tsp chilli powder

½ tsp mild curry powder,
    shopbought or see p.194
    (optional)

leaves from 2 or 3 little
    gem lettuces

To garnish

small bunch of coriander

small bunch of mint

1. Put the diced chicken and mango in a bowl and add the spring onions. Whisk together the soy or fish sauce with the lime juice and zest, chilli powder and curry powder, if using. Taste and season with salt and pepper. Pour this dressing over the chicken and stir thoroughly to combine.

2. To serve, spoon the chicken mixture on to little gem leaves and garnish with a few coriander and mint leaves.

DAVINA'S TIP: *This is a great dish to serve as a party snack or a starter and you can also take it to work or school with you. Just pile the filling into a box, wash a bunch of lettuce leaves and pop them in a bag, then you're good to go.*

Grilled Chicken, Asparagus and Courgette Salad

I love this salad and it's a great one to make for a party as well as for a picnic or packed lunch. There's protein, plenty of tasty veg and a tangy dressing and it's nice still warm from the pan or cold. If you're having this as a packed lunch, take the dressing in a separate pot and add it just before eating.

Serves 4

2 skinless chicken breasts

100g asparagus tips, split in half lengthways

1 courgette, cut into thin slices on the diagonal

zest and juice of 1 lemon

1 tbsp finely chopped tarragon leaves

½ tsp wholegrain mustard

100g baby leaf greens

150g cherry tomatoes, halved

mint and basil leaves, to garnish

1. First prepare the chicken. Lay one of the breasts on a chopping board, insert your knife at one side and cut through to the other side, keeping the knife parallel to the chopping board. Repeat with the other chicken breast to give you 4 pieces of chicken. Put each slice between 2 sheets of cling film and pound them with a meat mallet or rolling pin until they are nice and thin. Sprinkle the chicken with salt and pepper.

2. Heat a griddle pan until it is too hot to hold your hand over. Toss the asparagus and courgette in a tablespoon of olive oil and season them with salt and pepper. Cook the asparagus on the griddle pan for 3–4 minutes, shaking the pan regularly, until all the pieces are lightly charred all over, then remove and set aside. Add the slices of courgette to the pan and cook for 2–3 minutes on each side.

3. Turn the heat under the griddle down to medium, then grill the chicken for 1–2 minutes on each side. Check it is cooked through, then remove it from the pan and leave it to rest and cool. Cut the chicken into thin slices.

4. For the dressing, whisk 2 tablespoons of olive oil with the lemon zest and juice, tarragon and mustard. Season with salt and black pepper.

5. Put the salad leaves in a bowl (or portable containers) with the asparagus, courgette, chicken and tomatoes. When you're ready to eat, pour over the salad dressing and toss lightly. Serve garnished with a generous sprinkling of mint and basil leaves.

Chicken Drumsticks and Coleslaw

These two recipes make perfect partners for a packed lunch. Really sticky chicken drumsticks are notoriously messy, but this version is much easier for lunches on the go and still super yum. There are more than ten ingredients here but there are two recipes, which can be used separately.

Serves 4

Chicken drumsticks
zest of 1 lemon
1 garlic clove, crushed
1 tsp mild chilli powder
1 tsp dried oregano
8 chicken drumsticks
　　(or 12 chicken wings)

Coleslaw
½ small green cabbage,
　　very finely shredded
1 courgette, coarsely
　　grated
2 tsp white wine vinegar
6 spring onions, finely
　　chopped
1 tbsp mayonnaise
1 tbsp crème fraiche
zest and juice of 1 lime
a few tarragon leaves,
　　finely chopped

1. Preheat the oven to 200°C/Fan 180°C/Gas 6.

2. Mix the lemon zest, garlic, chilli powder and oregano in a bowl with 2 tablespoons of olive oil and season well with salt and pepper. Rub this mixture over the chicken pieces, getting as much under the skin as possible, then leave them in the fridge to marinate for at least an hour.

3. Roast the chicken in the oven for 35–40 minutes, until it's all crisp and rich golden brown.

4. To make the coleslaw, put the cabbage and the courgette into a colander. Sprinkle over half a teaspoon of salt and the white wine vinegar and toss gently, then leave the vegetables to stand for an hour. This will help get rid of any excess water and stops the coleslaw going soggy.

5. Tip the cabbage and courgette into a bowl and add the spring onions. Whisk the mayonnaise and crème fraiche together with the lime zest and juice, then stir in the tarragon leaves. Pour this dressing over the vegetables and mix thoroughly.

6. Serve the drumsticks with the coleslaw on the side.

I love cooking and I love eating but sometimes the tough bit is thinking what to have. Tuesday night inspiration?! It's tricky and I get stuck in a rut of making the same dishes over and over again. So I'm thrilled to have a great new bunch of supper recipes to share with you. There's some hearty soups, like winter minestrone, quick, cheap and cheerful dishes such as carbonara – with some extra veggies sneaked in – and chicken stir-fry, as well as some treats – try prawn pilaf, squash chilli and lamb flatbreads. Be brave, cook something new and don't ask the kids if they want it. Just give it to them. I told mine everything was chicken for a few years. Have fun making these recipes, be inspired as I was and I'd love to know how you get on. Keep in touch.

Family Suppers

Summer Minestrone

This is a beautifully fresh, light summery soup but with all the vegetables and the giant couscous (which you can find in supermarkets) it still makes a good nourishing meal. I like to keep it vegetarian but you can use chicken stock if you prefer the flavour.

Serves 4

15g butter

2 leeks, finely sliced

2 garlic cloves, finely chopped

1 litre vegetable stock

30g giant couscous

2 courgettes, sliced on the diagonal

200g asparagus, trimmed and cut into short lengths

200g runner or green beans, trimmed

100g peas or broad beans, (broad beans skinned if you like)

2 tomatoes, peeled and finely chopped

1. Heat the butter with a tablespoon of olive oil in a large saucepan. Add the leeks and garlic, put a lid on the pan and cook them very gently over a low heat for about 10 minutes.

2. Add the stock and giant couscous, season with salt and pepper, then simmer for 5 minutes. Add the courgettes, asparagus, beans and peas and simmer until all the vegetables are just tender – another 5–6 minutes. Stir in the tomatoes and simmer for 3–4 minutes.

DAVINA'S TIP: *If you like, you could add a swirl of red or green pesto (see p.192) when you serve the soup. Or add a few basil leaves and some grated Parmesan (or a vegetarian equivalent).*

Winter Minestrone

This is a really yummy, chunky, warming hug of a soup. It's good and hearty too so will fill you up and keep all the family happy. I keep it vegetarian but if you prefer, you can use a good chicken or ham stock instead of veggie stock. And if you have a rind of Parmesan (or vegetarian equivalent) lurking in the fridge, chuck it into the soup with the cabbage and it will add lots of flavour.

Serves 4

2 onions, thickly sliced

3 celery sticks, thickly sliced on the diagonal

2 large carrots, thickly sliced on the diagonal

2 garlic cloves, finely chopped

1 tsp dried mixed herbs

1 litre vegetable stock

400g can of borlotti or cannellini beans, drained

300g cavolo nero or savoy cabbage, shredded

2 tomatoes, peeled and finely chopped

50g cooked wholemeal pasta (optional)

1. Heat a tablespoon of olive oil in a large saucepan. Add the onions, celery and carrots and cook them over a medium heat, stirring regularly, until they have started to soften and caramelise around the edges. This can take a while – about 15 minutes.

2. Add the garlic, herbs, stock, beans and cabbage and season well with salt and pepper. If you do have a cheese rind, add this too. Bring the soup to the boil, then turn down the heat, cover the pan and simmer for 30 minutes until all the vegetables are tender.

3. Add the tomatoes and simmer for another 5 minutes, then add the pasta, if using, and let it heat through.

DAVINA'S TIP: *I like to add a drizzle of olive oil and some grated vegetarian Parmesan-style cheese to each bowlful when serving this soup.*

Mushroom Noodle Soup

This is a seriously simple, speedy soup. There's a Japanese vibe with the miso paste and the noodles, but don't worry – all these things are available in the supermarket and are very easy to use. This is a good recipe for vegetarians and vegans but do just check your soy sauce is suitable. Most are.

Serves 4

3–4 tbsp miso paste

30g fresh root ginger, finely sliced

2 garlic cloves, finely sliced

300g mixed mushrooms, larger ones sliced

200g Asian greens, shredded lengthways

1 tbsp soy sauce

100g wholewheat soba or udon noodles

1 tsp sesame oil

4 spring onions, halved lengthways and shredded, to garnish

1. Put the miso paste in a saucepan and pour over a litre of just-boiled water. Whisk until the miso is completely dissolved, then add the ginger and garlic. Simmer for 5 minutes, then add the mushrooms and greens. Continue to cook for a few more minutes until the vegetables are cooked through. Add the soy sauce and taste for seasoning – add some salt and pepper if you think the soup needs them.

2. Meanwhile, cook the noodles according to the instructions on the packet. Drain them thoroughly, then toss them with the sesame oil to stop them sticking together.

3. Pile the noodles into 4 bowls and ladle the soup over them. Garnish with the spring onions.

Chicken Harira

Harira is a traditional Moroccan soup and makes a really lovely comforting supper.
It's often made with lamb but my family prefer this lighter chicken version. It's mouthwateringly
good! I sometimes serve it with some brown rice on the side for everyone to add to their bowlful if
they like. A 50-gram serving of brown rice will add about 180 calories.

Serves 4

1 onion, finely chopped

1 garlic clove, finely
  chopped

600g chicken thigh
  fillets, diced

1 tbsp ras-el-hanout or
  Moroccan spice mix
  (see p.194)

pinch of saffron, soaked
  in a little warm water

400g can of chickpeas,
  drained

500ml chicken stock

400g can of chopped
  tomatoes

2 roasted red peppers
  (from a jar or see p.196),
  cut into strips

juice of 1 lemon

1. Heat a tablespoon of olive oil in a large saucepan. Add the onion and cook it over a medium to low heat until it's soft and translucent, then add the garlic and cook for a further 2 minutes.

2. Turn up the heat and add the diced chicken. Cook briskly until the chicken is lightly coloured on all sides, then sprinkle in the spice. Stir to combine, then add the saffron with its soaking water, the chickpeas, stock and tomatoes. Season with salt and pepper, bring to the boil, then turn down the heat and cover the pan. Simmer for half an hour until the chicken is very tender.

3. Add the red peppers and lemon juice and cook, uncovered, for a further 20 minutes until the soup has reduced down a little.

4. Great with or without some brown rice or wholemeal couscous.

My Carbonara

This is my go-to dish when everyone is starving and I need to get something filling and fabulous on the table fast. I've always loved a carbonara and this variation on the classic uses wholewheat pasta for plenty of fibre and includes some veg as well. Quick and super comforting.

Serves 4

250g wholewheat spaghetti

75g pancetta, diced

1 large courgette, coarsely grated

1 garlic clove, finely chopped

1 egg and 2 egg yolks

75g Parmesan or Pecorino cheese, grated

1. Bring a large saucepan of water to the boil, and add plenty of salt. Add the spaghetti and cook until it's just done but still has a little bite to it – this will take 10–12 minutes. Before draining, set aside a couple of ladlefuls of the cooking water.

2. Meanwhile, heat a teaspoon of olive oil in a frying pan that's large enough to hold the cooked pasta. Add the pancetta and cook until it's crisp and most of the fat has rendered out. Remove the pancetta from the pan and set it aside. Add the courgette and garlic and cook for 2–3 minutes, then take the pan off the heat.

3. Beat the egg and egg yolks in a bowl with the cheese until the eggs are well broken up. Add the cooked pasta to the frying pan with the courgette and garlic, then pour over the egg mixture and about 50ml of the pasta cooking water. Cook in the residual heat of the pan, swirling the pasta around until it's all coated in the creamy sauce. Add a little more water if necessary, then stir in the cooked pancetta.

4. Divide between 4 bowls and serve immediately.

Miso-braised Aubergines

This makes a nice starter on its own or could be served as a main course, perhaps with some wilted greens and brown rice or noodles. Quite sophisticated flavours so maybe best for a grown-up supper.

Serves 4

2 large aubergines, cut in half lengthways

1 tbsp miso paste

1 tbsp rice wine vinegar

1 tbsp mirin

30g fresh root ginger, grated

sesame seeds

2 spring onions, cut in half lengthways and shredded into thin matchsticks

1. Take each aubergine half and score a diamond pattern through the flesh, making sure you don't cut through to the skin. This will help the heat and flavour get right into the aubergine. Sprinkle the cut side with salt.

2. Heat 2 tablespoons of vegetable oil in a frying pan or a flameproof casserole dish that has a lid and is large enough to hold all of the aubergines. Fry the aubergine halves, cut-side down, for about 5–6 minutes over a medium heat until the flesh is richly coloured, then carefully turn them over. Cover the pan and continue to fry the aubergines for a further 5 minutes or until they are completely cooked through.

3. Preheat your grill to a medium to high setting. Mix together the miso paste, vinegar, mirin and ginger. If the mixture seems too thick, add a few drops of water, then brush it over the cut side of the aubergines. Put the aubergines under the grill for 4–5 minutes until the miso glaze is hot and bubbling.

4. Sprinkle the aubergines with sesame seeds and spring onions and serve.

Thai Vegetable Curry

I call this easy-peasy Thai curry – it's so simple to put together and you can use whatever veggies you have handy in the fridge. It makes a great vegetarian supper and if you leave out the fish sauce it would be fine for vegans too. This one is going to be a regular in our household.

Serves 4

400ml coconut milk

400ml vegetable stock

2–3 tbsp Thai curry paste (shopbought or see p.195)

400g salad potatoes

as many as you like of the following veg: butternut squash, mangetout, sprouting broccoli, baby corn, asparagus stems, small courgettes, sugar snap peas

juice of 1 lime

2 Kaffir lime leaves, shredded

1–2 tbsp fish sauce

coriander leaves, to garnish

 (leave out fish sauce)

1. Pour the coconut milk into a saucepan and add the vegetable stock or the same amount of water. Add 2 tablespoons of curry paste. Bring to the boil, then turn down the heat and add the potatoes and squash, if using. Season with salt and simmer for 10 minutes.

2. Cut the remaining vegetables into bite-sized pieces and add them to the curry with the lime juice, lime leaves and a tablespoon of fish sauce. Simmer until just tender – this will take about 5 minutes.

3. Taste, then add another tablespoon of curry paste and of fish sauce if you like and season with salt and pepper. Sprinkle with coriander leaves and serve. Brown rice is nice with this if you want some carbs.

Cauliflower and Broccoli Salad

This is a nice substantial salad and a really good vegan dish. There's protein, fibre and lots of flavour – ticks all the boxes for me. It's super quick to make with ready-cooked or leftover lentils but if you want to cook some yourself, see my tip on page 60.

Serves 4

½ cauliflower, separated into small florets

1 head of broccoli, separated into small florets

2 tbsp flaked almonds

150g cooked green or brown lentils

100g baby salad leaves

Tahini dressing

150g tahini

zest and juice of 1 lemon

½ tsp cinnamon

small bunch of parsley, finely chopped, a few reserved to garnish

small bunch of mint, finely chopped, a few leaves reserved to garnish

1. Preheat the oven to 200°C/Fan 180°C/Gas 6. Put the cauliflower and broccoli in a roasting tin and drizzle over 2 tablespoons of olive oil. Season with salt and pepper. Roast the vegetables for 30–35 minutes until they're lightly charred around the edges and just tender.

2. Put the almonds into a dry frying pan and toast them over a medium heat until lightly coloured, shaking the pan regularly.

3. To make the dressing, stir the tahini thoroughly before spooning some out of the jar, as it does tend to separate. Put the tahini in a bowl and whisk in 100ml of warm water and the lemon zest and juice. Add the cinnamon and season with salt and pepper, then stir thoroughly and taste – add more seasoning or lemon juice if you think it needs it. Add the herbs, setting aside a few leaves for the garnish. Blitz the dressing in a food processor if you want it to be very smooth, otherwise just stir the herbs through.

4. Serve the roasted broccoli and cauliflower with the cooked lentils and leaves. Drizzle over the dressing, then garnish with the reserved herbs and the flaked almonds.

American-style Squash Chilli

My family likes a chilli and I love this version with lots of veggies. You can make it as spicy, or not, as you like and non-vegetarians can enjoy a slice of cornbread too (see page 90). Sooooo delish!

Serves 4

1 onion, finely chopped

2 celery sticks, diced

2 red peppers, deseeded and diced

3 garlic cloves, finely chopped

1 tsp chilli powder (whatever you fancy – cayenne, chipotle, mild)

1 tsp dried sage and 1 tsp dried thyme

750g squash or pumpkin, cut into 3cm dice

200ml vegetable stock (optional)

200g fresh or canned tomatoes, peeled and chopped

1 large bunch of spring greens, kale or cavolo nero, thickly shredded

V (without cornbread)

1. Heat a tablespoon of olive oil in a wide frying pan that has a lid. Add the onion, celery and peppers with a splash of water. Cover the pan and cook the veg over a low heat for 10 minutes, then stir in the garlic, chilli powder, sage and thyme.

2. Stir to combine, then add the squash. Add the vegetable stock, or the same amount of water, and the tomatoes. Season with salt and pepper. Bring to the boil, then turn down the heat and simmer until the squash is tender – this will take about 15 minutes.

3. Wash the greens thoroughly and put them in a large saucepan with the water that's clinging to the leaves. Cook the greens until just tender, then drain and stir them into the squash. Simmer the chilli uncovered to reduce the sauce a little, then serve.

Sweetcorn and Bacon Cornbread

This is perfect served with the squash chilli on page 89 to soak up all the lovely juices, but it's also good with a bowl of soup for lunch. If you want a vegetarian version, leave out the bacon but stir in two tablespoons of olive oil with the sweetcorn.

Makes 16 squares

100g diced bacon
250g medium cornmeal (polenta)
100g wholemeal flour (wheat or spelt)
1 tbsp baking powder
½ tsp bicarbonate of soda
2 large eggs
400ml buttermilk
200g sweetcorn (freshly hulled or defrosted)

1. Preheat the oven to 220°C/Fan 200°C/Gas 7. Heat 2 tablespoons of olive oil in a frying pan and fry the bacon until it's crisp and brown. Remove the bacon with a slotted spoon and put it in a bowl, then pour any oil and bacon fat left in the frying pan into a 20cm-square baking tin.

2. Put all the dry ingredients in a large bowl and add half a teaspoon of salt. Whisk thoroughly to combine. Beat the eggs lightly, then mix them into the buttermilk. Make a well in the middle of the dry ingredients and pour in the egg and buttermilk mixture. Mix everything together, then stir in the bacon and sweetcorn.

3. Scrape the batter into the tin and smooth the top with a palette knife. Bake the cornbread in the oven for about 15 minutes, until well risen and golden-brown around the edges. Remove it from the oven, cut into about 16 squares and serve hot.

Fish with Lemon and Orange Butter Sauce

The tangy, buttery sauce makes this fish dish something really special and I find that children really love the flavours. Defo a regular for my household.

Serves 4

4 fillets of sea bass or
   similar white fish
½ tsp ground cardamom
¼ tsp ground cinnamon
¼ tsp cayenne
2 tbsp butter
1 garlic clove, crushed
finely grated zest and juice
   of 2 lemons
juice of 1 orange or
   2 mandarins

1. Pat the sea bass fillets dry. Mix the cardamom, cinnamon and cayenne with a good pinch of salt and some ground black or white pepper. Sprinkle this mixture evenly over both sides of the fish.

2. Heat a tablespoon of olive oil in a large frying pan. When it's hot, add the sea bass fillets skin-side down. Fry them for 2–3 minutes until the skin is crisp and you can see that the flesh around the edges is turning opaque. Carefully turn the fillets over and cook them for a further minute. Remove them from the pan and keep them warm.

3. Add the butter, garlic, lemon zest and juice and the orange juice to the pan and season with salt and pepper. Turn up the heat and simmer until the sauce is reduced to a syrupy consistency.

4. Serve the fish with the sauce and perhaps some steamed new potatoes and green beans or broccoli or just a salad.

Greek Baked Prawns

This classic Greek dish of prawns and feta (prawn saganaki) is a great winter warmer. The ouzo (Greek aniseed-flavoured aperitif) does add a nice bit of flavour but if you don't have any, the dish will still taste great. Serve with salad and sourdough bread for dipping into the sauce or over pasta. Super-good whichever way. Yassou! (That's a way of saying hello in Greek, BTW.)

Serves 4

1 onion, finely chopped

5 garlic cloves, crushed or grated

small bunch of basil, shredded, a few whole leaves reserved to garnish

small bunch of parsley, finely chopped

500g ripe tomatoes, peeled and chopped

pinch of cinnamon

1 tbsp ouzo (optional)

12 large prawns, peeled and deveined

300g feta, crumbled or cubed

1. Heat a tablespoon of olive oil in a shallow, ovenproof pan. Add the onion and cook it gently until very soft. Add 3 of the garlic cloves, and continue to cook for another 2–3 minutes.

2. Add the shredded basil, the parsley and tomatoes. Season with salt and pepper and add the pinch of cinnamon, then bring to the boil. Once the sauce is boiling, add the ouzo, if using, then turn down the heat, put a lid on the pan and leave the sauce to simmer and reduce for 10 minutes. Preheat your grill to a medium to high setting.

3. Toss the prawns in a tablespoon of olive oil and the remaining garlic and season them with salt and pepper. Sprinkle the feta over the tomato sauce, then top with the prawns. Put the pan under the grill for 5–6 minutes until the prawns are cooked through and the feta has softened and is lightly coloured in places.

4. Sprinkle with the reserved basil leaves and serve immediately.

    DAVINA'S TIP: *To make this an extra speedy dish, you can use a quarter portion of the tomato sauce recipe on p.123 if you have some in the fridge or freezer, instead of making the sauce above. Heat it up and add the ouzo, if using, then add the feta and prawns and finish as above.*

Prawn Pilaf

Prawns are a favourite of mine and this pilaf makes a great one-pot dish. There's protein, good wholegrain carbs and vegetables, so everything you need for a yummy supper.

Serves 4

250g brown basmati rice

1 onion, finely chopped

2 garlic cloves, finely chopped

1 tbsp mild curry powder (shopbought or see p.194)

zest and juice of 1 lime

500ml vegetable or chicken stock

500g peeled raw prawns, deveined

1 large courgette, finely chopped

3 little gem lettuces, shredded

chopped mint, coriander, parsley, dill (as many or as few as you like), to serve

1. Put the rice in a bowl, cover it with cold water and leave it to soak for 15 minutes. Drain it thoroughly and set aside.

2. Heat a tablespoon of olive oil in a large saucepan or a flameproof casserole dish and add the onion. Cook it until soft and translucent, then add the garlic, curry powder, lime zest and rice. Cook and stir for 2–3 minutes until the rice is coated with the spices, then pour in the stock. Season with salt and pepper.

3. Bring to the boil, cover the pan, and cook the rice over a high heat for 5 minutes. Turn the heat down and continue to cook for a further 20 minutes. At this point, most of the liquid should be absorbed by the rice and it should be almost al dente.

4. Season the prawns with salt and half the lime juice. Lay the courgette, lettuce and prawns on top of the rice, then cover the pan. Continue to cook, allowing the prawns to steam, for a further 5 minutes until the rice is tender and the prawns are pink and cooked through.

5. Taste for seasoning and add the remaining lime juice if necessary. Stir through the herbs before serving.

Roasted Fish with Lime Tartare

Baking fish is so easy and these fillets with their crispy crunchy topping are seriously good. The lime tartare is the perfect accompaniment, then all you need is a salad and perhaps some new potatoes for a speedy supper.

Serves 4

4–8 skinned white fish fillets

2 limes

25g Cheddar or Gruyère cheese, grated

25g brown breadcrumbs

a few basil leaves

25g butter

25g mayonnaise

75g crème fraiche

4 small cornichons, finely chopped

2 tbsp capers, rinsed and finely chopped (optional)

1. Preheat the oven to 200°C/Fan 180°C/Gas 6. Line a baking tray with non-stick baking paper.

2. Season the fish with salt, then arrange the pieces on the baking tray. Mix the zest of one of the limes with the cheese, breadcrumbs and some of the basil leaves and season. Spread this mixture evenly over the fish. Melt the butter and drizzle it over the topping.

3. Put the baking tray in the oven and bake the fish for 15 minutes or until it is cooked through (the exact time will depend on the thickness of the fish) and the topping is crisp and brown.

4. While the fish is roasting, make the tartare. Mix the mayonnaise and crème fraiche in a bowl and add the cornichons, capers, zest of the remaining lime, a tablespoon of lime juice and a few shredded basil leaves. Season with salt and pepper. Serve the fish with the tartare on the side.

Trout and Watercress Salad

Smoked trout is an old fave of mine and makes a simple salad into a nourishing meal.
Try this yummy recipe and I'm sure you'll enjoy it as much as I do.

Serves 4

100g green beans,
    trimmed

2 oranges

100g watercress, large
    stems removed

½ cucumber, sliced into
    ribbons

4 cold smoked trout fillets

a few dill sprigs

a few mint leaves

juice of ½ lemon

1. Bring a saucepan of water to the boil and add the green beans. Blanch them for 3–4 minutes until just tender – they should still be a bright, fresh green. Drain and run them under cold water, then set aside.

2. Cut off thin slices from the top and bottom of one of the oranges, then stand it upright. Cut away the skin and membrane, following the curve of the sides. Take the orange in your hand and hold it over a bowl. Cut away the segments as close to the membranes as you can, flicking out any pips as you go. Squeeze out the membranes before discarding. Do this with the peel too – there will be a lot of juice, which will be nice in the dressing. Repeat to segment the other orange.

3. To assemble the salad, arrange the beans, watercress and cucumber in a serving dish. Break up the trout fillets and add them too, then follow with the orange segments and herbs.

4. For the dressing, mix the lemon juice with 2 tablespoons of olive oil and the saved orange juice, then season with salt and pepper. Whisk thoroughly, then drizzle the dressing over the salad. Serve immediately.

Skate Wings with Salsa Verde

I didn't used to be very adventurous with fish but now I've discovered skate wings and I think they're fantastic. They're not as expensive as some fish, they're simple to cook and my children love them because there are no bones – the flesh peels away very easily. Capers are a traditional partner for skate so this zesty herby salsa verde is just right. Add some green salad and a few new potatoes and you have a feast. You can also use ray wings for this dish.

Serves 4

4 skate wings, about
    250g each
a few thyme leaves
4 branches of cherry
    tomatoes on the vine

Salsa verde
50g can of anchovies
zest and juice of 1 lemon
small bunch of parsley,
    finely chopped
small bunch of basil,
    leaves only, finely
    shredded
2 tbsp capers, rinsed

1. First make the salsa verde. Put the anchovies and their oil in a small saucepan and add 2 tablespoons of olive oil and the lemon zest and juice. Put the pan over a medium heat and keep breaking up the anchovies with a wooden spoon until they have blended with the oil and lemon. Taste for seasoning – you may not need any salt, but add some pepper. Leave the sauce to one side until you are ready to serve the fish, then stir in the herbs and capers.

2. Preheat the oven to 200°C/Fan 180°C/Gas 6. Line a roasting tin with non-stick baking paper and brush it with a little olive oil.

3. Trim the wings so they can fit in a single layer in the tin – use scissors to cut away any edges of the wings that you can see don't have any flesh on them. Season the wings with salt and pepper and place them in the roasting tin. Brush them with a little more olive oil and sprinkle with the thyme leaves.

4. Bake the wings in the oven for 5 minutes, then add the tomatoes. Continue to bake for a further 6–7 minutes until the fish is just cooked through and the tomatoes are close to bursting point. Serve the fish and tomatoes with the sauce spooned over them.

Mediterranean Fish Casserole

Another recipe with everything you need all in one pot. I do love these sort of suppers where you don't end up feeling like you've used every pan in the kitchen. Makes it all taste even better somehow – and there are fewer arguments about the clearing up!

Serves 4

1 large or 2 small fennel bulbs

300g new potatoes, skins on, halved

2 garlic cloves, finely chopped

zest and juice of 1 lemon

small bunch of parsley, finely chopped

1 pinch of saffron, soaked in a little water

300ml fish stock

200g tomatoes, peeled and chopped

1 courgette, cut into slices, on the diagonal

500g skinless fish fillets, cut into large chunks (cod, haddock, etc)

1. Heat 2 tablespoons of olive oil in a large flameproof casserole dish. Trim the fennel, then cut it into thick slices or wedges. Add these to the pan and fry them over a fairly high heat until they're starting to caramelise around the edges.

2. Add the potatoes to the pan and continue to cook for several minutes, stirring regularly. Add the garlic, lemon zest and parsley (setting aside 2 tablespoons for the garnish), then pour in the saffron and fish stock. Season with salt and pepper.

3. Bring to the boil, then turn down the heat and cover the pan. Simmer for 10–12 minutes, until the fennel and potatoes are tender, then add the tomatoes and courgette. Put the fish fillets on top, then cover the pan again and simmer, allowing the fish to steam until it is cooked through. It shouldn't take more than 3–4 minutes. Add lemon juice to taste.

4. Serve the casserole in shallow bowls with the reserved parsley sprinkled over the top.

Penne and Sausage Bake

It took my family a little while to get used to wholewheat pasta but now we have it all the time and we love it. Lots of veggies and little balls of sausage makes this an A-M-A-ZING one-pot supper that leaves everyone smiling. And if you have the tomato sauce already made it's quick too.

Serves 6

250g squash or pumpkin, peeled and diced

1 tsp dried sage

6 sausages, skinned and rolled into balls

200g wholewheat penne

200g sprouting broccoli, roughly chopped

500ml tomato sauce (see p.123)

100ml single cream

1 mozzarella ball (125g)

1. Preheat the oven to 200°C/Fan 180°C/Gas 6. Put the squash in a large roasting tin and season it with salt and pepper. Drizzle over a tablespoon of olive oil and sprinkle the sage over the squash. Roast the squash in the oven for 20 minutes, then add the sausage balls to the tin and cook for another 10 minutes.

2. Meanwhile, bring a large saucepan of water to the boil and add salt. Add the penne and cook for 8 minutes, then add the sprouting broccoli. Continue to cook until both are done but still have a little bite to them – this should take another 3–4 minutes. Drain thoroughly.

3. Put the pasta and broccoli in a large ovenproof dish. Mix the tomato sauce with the cream and stir it into the pasta and broccoli until well combined. Add the squash and sausage and lightly push them into the pasta mixture. Pull apart the mozzarella and scatter it over the top.

4. Bake in the oven for 20–25 minutes until the pasta is bubbling and the mozzarella has melted and started to turn golden brown.

Chicken Stir-fry

Stir-fries are the ultimate in quick suppers so they're a regular in our house where speed is all-important much of the time. This recipe has a lovely tangy, citrusy sauce and can be served with or without brown rice or noodles, depending on whether you're counting carbs or not.

Serves 4

400g sprouting broccoli, cut into lengths

600g chicken breast or thigh fillets, cut into strips

⅓ tsp chilli flakes (optional)

100ml chicken stock

2 tbsp soy sauce

juice of 2 lemons

juice of 1 orange

2 garlic cloves, crushed or grated

2 tsp cornflour

To serve

brown rice or wholemeal noodles (optional)

1. Heat a tablespoon of vegetable oil in a wok. When it is very hot and the air above it is shimmering, add the sprouting broccoli and cook, stirring constantly, until it is just al dente, but still bright green. Remove the broccoli from the wok with a slotted spoon and set it aside.

2. Make sure the wok is still very hot and add a little more vegetable oil if necessary. Add the chicken and chilli flakes, if using, and cook for about 3 minutes, until the chicken strips are coloured on all sides.

3. Mix together the chicken stock, soy sauce, lemon and orange juice and garlic, then pour this over the chicken. Return the broccoli to the wok and simmer for a couple of minutes. Mix the cornflour with a little cold water, making sure it is completely lump free, then add this to the wok. Simmer for another minute or so, stirring constantly, until the sauce thickens slightly.

4. Serve this on its own for a low-carb option or with brown rice or noodles. Fifty grams of brown rice or wholewheat noodles will add about 180 calories to your total.

Lamb Flatbreads

The flatbreads for this recipe are made with baking powder, not yeast, so they don't take so long to prove. They are fun to make and children will enjoy adding the toppings – feel free to vary as you like.

Makes 4

150g wholemeal flour
(wheat or spelt), plus
extra for dusting
1½ tsp baking powder
150ml yoghurt

Topping
2 tbsp tomato purée
½ tsp chilli flakes or
powder
½ tsp cinnamon
1 garlic clove, crushed
200g lean lamb mince
1 roasted red pepper,
peeled and pulled into
strips (peppers from a
jar are fine or see p.196)
2 tbsp pine nuts
rocket leaves and lemon
wedges, to serve

1. To make the dough, mix together the flour and baking powder with half a teaspoon of salt. Stir in the yoghurt and mix to make a slightly sticky dough. Form the dough into a ball, put it in a bowl and cover with cling film or a damp tea towel. Leave it to stand at room temperature for about an hour.

2. Preheat the oven to its highest temperature – at least 220°C/Fan 200°C/Gas 7.

3. For the topping, mix the tomato purée with the chilli flakes or powder, cinnamon and garlic. Stir in the minced lamb and season well with salt and pepper.

4. To assemble, divide the dough into 4 pieces and roll each piece out as thinly as possible on a well-floured surface. You can make rounds about 18cm in diameter or teardrop shapes if you prefer. Dust 2 upturned baking trays with flour and put 2 flatbreads on each. Divide the topping mixture between the 4 flatbreads, then top with strips of red pepper. Sprinkle over the pine nuts.

5. Cook the flatbreads in the oven for 8–10 minutes until the dough is a light golden brown and the lamb is cooked. Remove them from the oven. Season the rocket leaves and drizzle them with olive oil, then divide them between the flatbreads. Serve immediately with lemon wedges for squeezing over the top.

DAVINA'S TIP: *This dough freezes well so you can make double quantities if you like. Divide it into individual portions and wrap well. Defrost by leaving the dough at room temperature until soft and pliable, then roll as before.*

Lamb and Chickpea Salad

I do like dishes that use a small amount of meat to add flavour and oomph to a dish. This warm salad makes a couple of lamb steaks go a long way with the help of some chickpeas and greens. You could also make it with some leftover roast lamb – just cut it into strips and lightly char it in a pan.

Serves 4

2 lamb steaks (about 200g in total)
large bag of lamb's lettuce
½ cucumber, sliced into ribbons
400g can of chickpeas, drained
1 lemon
a few mint leaves, to garnish

Dressing

pinch of saffron strands soaked in a little warm water
100ml yoghurt
juice of 1 lemon
1 tsp honey (optional)

1. Heat a griddle pan until it is too hot to hold your hand over comfortably. Season the lamb with salt and pepper on both sides. Grill the lamb for 2–3 minutes on each side until the surface is marked with char lines but the meat is still pink. Remove the lamb from the pan and leave it to rest for 10 minutes, then slice it into thin strips.

2. To make the dressing, add the saffron and its soaking water to the yoghurt, along with the lemon juice and the honey, if using. Whisk thoroughly until the yoghurt has turned a sunny yellow, then season generously with salt and pepper. Thin the dressing with a little water if you think it needs it.

3. To assemble the salad, arrange the lamb's lettuce, cucumber and chickpeas over a large platter or in 4 individual shallow bowls. Drizzle over a tablespoon of olive oil and squeeze over some lemon juice, then toss lightly. Add the lamb, then drizzle over the dressing and garnish with a few mint leaves.

Beef and Mushroom Stir-fry

You'll find wholewheat egg noodles in most supermarkets and they work really well for this fab and super-speedy stir-fry. This is another great way of making a small amount of meat go a long way and so makes a relatively inexpensive supper.

Serves 4

4 nests of wholewheat egg noodles

a few drops of sesame oil

200g frying steak, sliced into strips

½ tsp Chinese five-spice powder

1 red pepper, cut into strips

300g chestnut mushrooms, or a mixture, halved or sliced if very large

30g fresh root ginger, finely sliced into matchsticks

2 garlic cloves, finely chopped

200g oriental greens

1–2 tbsp soy sauce

1. Bring a large saucepan of water to the boil and add salt. Add the noodles and cook them for 5 minutes. Drain the noodles, then toss them in a little sesame oil.

2. Put the strips of steak in a bowl and toss them with the five-spice powder. Heat a tablespoon of vegetable oil in a wok. When the oil has started to smoke, or the air above it has started to shimmer, add the steak. Cook the strips very quickly, stirring them until they are browned on all sides but still pink in the middle. Scoop the steak strips out of the wok and transfer them to a plate to rest.

3. Let the oil get really hot again, then add the red pepper and mushrooms. Stir-fry them for 3–4 minutes, then add the ginger, garlic and greens. Pour in the soy sauce and any juices from the resting beef and continue to cook until the greens have wilted. Add the noodles and steak and warm everything through for a minute or so. Serve at once.

DAVINA'S TIP: *I like to garnish this dish with a few shredded spring onions, and a sprinkling of sesame seeds and fresh mint or coriander leaves.*

There are a couple of speedy recipes on the following pages, such as chicken fried rice and chickpea and chard curry, and others that are all about saving time (and money) by batch cooking. A little time spent making a load of tomato sauce, baked beans or Italian-style meat sauce really yields dividends. It's such a great feeling when you can pull something out of the freezer in the morning, knowing that means dinner is almost done come the evening. Love it! Roast chicken is one of my favourite treats and in this chapter I suggest how that one meal can be stretched to three, using every bit of your bird.

Save Time, Save Money

Simple Dal

Dal is a beautifully warming, comforting dish and this is a very simple, easy-to-make version with a nice onion garnish to stir in at the end. It makes a really cheap supper with a salad or veggies on the side or you can serve it with another curry. The texture should be quite soupy.

Serves 4

1 onion, very finely
  chopped
30g fresh root ginger,
  grated
3 garlic cloves, crushed
  or grated
2 tsp cumin seeds
1 tsp ground turmeric
250g red lentils or chana
  dal (yellow split peas)

Fried onion garnish

2 tsp cumin seeds
1 onion, finely sliced

To serve

a few coriander leaves
lime wedges, for squeezing

1. Heat 2 tablespoons of vegetable oil or olive oil in a large saucepan. Add the onion and cook it over a medium heat until softened and starting to caramelise around the edges. Add the ginger, garlic and cumin seeds and continue to cook for 2–3 minutes. Stir in the turmeric and season generously.

2. Wash the lentils thoroughly until the water runs clear, then add them to the saucepan. Stir to coat the lentils with all the flavours, then add 900ml of just-boiled water. Bring to the boil and skim off any foam that forms, then turn down the heat and cover the pan. Simmer for 25–30 minutes, until the lentils have broken down. Taste for seasoning and add salt and pepper if necessary.

3. For the fried onion garnish, heat 2 tablespoons of vegetable oil in a frying pan over a medium heat and add the cumin seeds. Cook for a scant half minute, then add the onion. Cook gently until the slices have softened and lightly caramelised, while still keeping their shape. Season with salt and pepper and cook for another 2–3 minutes, then tip the onion on to kitchen paper to drain.

4. Serve the dal with the onion garnish, coriander leaves and lime wedges.

   DAVINA'S TIP: *For those who like a bit of extra heat, add a few sliced green chillies to the dal when you serve it.*

Italian-style Meat Sauce

It's well worth cooking a big batch of this version of Italian ragù and freezing some if you don't need it all at once. It's no more trouble to cook extra and saves you loads of time in the end. I've added lots of vegetables and some lentils to this recipe to eke out the meat and I really love the creamy texture that the lentils bring.

Serves about 8

400g lean minced beef

1 onion, finely chopped

200g each of 3 of the following: celery, carrot, swede, celeriac, squash, sweet potato, courgette, finely diced

2 garlic cloves, finely chopped

2 tsp mixed herbs or herbes de Provence

250ml red or white wine

250ml beef stock

250g cooked brown lentils

400g can of chopped tomatoes

1. Heat a tablespoon of olive oil in a large saucepan. Add the minced beef, breaking it up with the back of a wooden spoon, and sear it on all sides. Add the onion and other vegetables to the pan and fry them gently over a medium heat until they are starting to soften. Add the garlic and herbs and cook for a further 2–3 minutes.

2. Pour in the wine and bring it to the boil. Let the wine bubble until well reduced, then add the stock, lentils and tomatoes. Season generously and bring everything back to the boil.

3. Now turn the heat down to a simmer and cover the pan. Leave to cook for at least 45 minutes until the vegetables are tender and the sauce is a rich ochre colour. Then remove the lid from the pan and continue to simmer, uncovered, for a further 15 minutes to reduce the sauce down a little.

DAVINA'S TIP: *There are so many ways you can use this delish sauce – with pasta, as a base for a cottage pie or just on its own with boiled new potatoes and green vegetables or salad.*

Tomato Sauce

A good tomato sauce is one of the most useful things to have in your fridge or freezer. I know you can buy sauces in jars but making your own saves you loads of money – and having sauce available for quick suppers saves you precious time as well. And obvs, home-made is way better. Use this sauce over pasta, for lasagne, bean dishes, whatever you fancy.

Makes 1.5 litres

2 onions, very finely diced
½ bulb of garlic, cloves peeled and finely chopped
4 x 400g cans of chopped tomatoes
1 bay leaf
1 tbsp dried oregano
sprig of fresh thyme
pinch of cinnamon (optional)

1. Heat 4 tablespoons of olive oil in a heavy-based saucepan. Add the onions and fry them gently over a low to medium heat until they're very soft and translucent – this will take at least 15 minutes. Add the garlic and continue to cook for another 5 minutes.

2. Pour in the tomatoes along with 500ml of water – use the water to rinse out the cans, then add it to the sauce to make sure you use every bit of the tomatoes. Add the bay, oregano and thyme and season with salt and pepper. Bring the sauce to the boil, then turn down the heat, cover the pan, and leave to simmer for an hour. Stir regularly to make sure the sauce isn't catching on the base of the pan.

3. Remove the lid and taste the sauce. If it is at all acidic, add a generous pinch of cinnamon – this will provide a natural sweetness so is a good alternative to sugar. Continue to simmer for another half hour to reduce the sauce.

4. Take the pan off the heat and fish out the bay leaf and the thyme – all the leaves from the sprig will have dropped off into the sauce. If not using the sauce immediately, leave it to cool to room temperature before storing it in the fridge. It will keep for a week in the fridge or you can divide it into portions and pop them into the freezer.

Barley Risotto

Barley is a really nutritious grain and makes a great risotto. It's also half the price of risotto rice so it's good for your budget and your body. This recipe is packed with green veg too, so defo makes a good contribution to your five a day.

Serves 4

15g butter
2 leeks, finely sliced
2 garlic cloves, finely chopped
1 sprig of fresh thyme
200g pearl barley
1 litre hot vegetable stock
500g sprouting broccoli
1 large courgette, diced
100g peas
25g vegetarian Parmesan-style cheese, grated

1. Heat a tablespoon of olive oil with the butter in a large saucepan, then add the leeks. Sauté them over a gentle heat until they're soft and translucent, then stir in the garlic, thyme and barley. Stir until the barley looks glossy.

2. Pour in the stock and bring it to the boil. Season with salt and pepper. Turn down the heat and simmer gently for about 25 minutes or until the barley is cooked, stirring every so often to make sure it isn't catching on the base of the pan.

3. Meanwhile, put a small amount of water in a separate pan. Add the sprouting broccoli. Simmer until just tender, then drain thoroughly. When the barley is cooked through and most of the liquid has been absorbed, stir in the broccoli, courgette and peas. Heat through until everything is piping hot.

4. Add the grated cheese and beat it into the risotto until the mixture is lovely and creamy.

DAVINA'S TIP: *I like to add a sprinkling of lemon zest to this just before serving – brings all the flavours alive!*

Vegan Baked Beans

I'm cooking more and more vegan dishes and I'm liking this way of eating. This recipe makes a lovely big pot of beans and you can freeze any leftovers. Baked beans are always the most comforting of suppers and this version contains plenty of vegetables as well. Yummiest of the yummiest.

Serves 6

1 large onion, finely
   chopped

2 celery sticks, finely
   chopped

2 carrots, finely chopped

150g white button
   mushrooms, roughly
   chopped

150g sweet potato,
   pumpkin or squash,
   diced

4 garlic cloves, finely
   chopped

1 tbsp mixed herbs

400g can of tomatoes

1–2 tsp Marmite (to taste)

4 x 400g cans of haricot
   or cannellini beans,
   drained, or 1kg cooked
   white beans

1. Heat 2 tablespoons of olive oil in a large saucepan, then add the onion, celery, carrots and mushrooms. Cook them all over a fairly high heat, stirring regularly, until they have softened and caramelised. You will find that they will initially give out a fair amount of liquid, but be patient and allow this to evaporate off before expecting the vegetables to start browning.

2. Add the sweet potato or squash, garlic cloves and herbs. Continue to cook for another 5 minutes to give the sweet potatoes a chance to start browning. Season generously with salt and pepper.

3. Add the tomatoes, then rinse the can out with 200ml of water and add it to the saucepan. Bring to the boil, then turn the heat down and cover the pan. Simmer for 15 minutes, then remove the lid and continue to simmer until the sauce has reduced a little.

4. Take the pan off the heat and purée the sauce with a stick blender until smooth. Add a teaspoon of Marmite and stir to combine, then taste and add more Marmite if you like. Add the beans and stir to mix them into the sauce, then put the pan back on the heat to heat through before serving. These beans are great on their own or as a side dish.

DAVINA'S TIP: *Another delish (but non-vegan) way of enjoying these is to pile the beans into an ovenproof dish, add a topping of breadcrumbs and grated cheese and bake until the topping is golden and crunchy.*

Chickpea and Chard Curry

Quick and delicious, this one ticks all the boxes for my family. Sometimes I love a recipe that contains mostly store cupboard ingredients with just a few extras to pick up from the shops. Nice served with some brown rice or just a lovely crunchy salad.

Serves 4

1 red onion, thickly sliced

1 large bunch of Swiss chard, stems and leaves separated, shredded

1 red pepper, cut into strips

2 garlic cloves, finely chopped

1 tbsp mild curry powder

400ml can of coconut milk

200g canned tomatoes, puréed

2 x 400g cans of chickpeas, drained

small bunch of coriander leaves, finely chopped (optional), to serve

1. Heat a tablespoon of vegetable, coconut or olive oil in a large saucepan. Add the onion, chard stems and red pepper and cook over a medium heat until they start to soften.

2. Add the garlic and curry powder and cook for a further 2–3 minutes. Pour in the coconut milk, tomatoes, chickpeas, chard leaves and 200ml of water. Season with salt and pepper, then simmer until the greens have wilted down and the vegetables are tender. Stir in the coriander leaves, if using, just before serving.

Pot-roast Chicken

This is the perfect Sunday dinner – and all in one pot too! I do love a roast chicken and cooking it like this with all the vegetables is so easy. Enjoy your roast, save any leftovers to make a dish such as chicken fried rice (page 133), then use the carcass to make amazing chicken soup (page 134). Three family meals from one chicken – how's that for good budgeting!

Serves 4

1 chicken (about 1.5kg)

½ lemon

2 carrots, cut into chunks

1 fennel bulb, cut into wedges, lengthways

2 leeks, cut into large chunks

12 small new potatoes

250ml white wine

2 bay leaves

1 sprig of tarragon

6 garlic cloves, unpeeled

1 tbsp butter

1. Remove the chicken from the fridge an hour before you want to roast it so it has time to come up to room temperature. Preheat the oven to 200°C/Fan 180°C/Gas 6. Pat the chicken dry and rub it with a tablespoon of olive oil. Squeeze over the juice from the lemon half, then put it in the cavity of the chicken.

2. Arrange the vegetables in the base of a large flameproof casserole dish or a roasting tin and season them with salt and pepper. Pour over the wine and 100ml of water and tuck the herbs and garlic cloves in among the vegetables. Place the chicken on top.

3. Cover the dish with a lid or a double layer of foil and cook the chicken in the oven for 50 minutes. Remove the dish from the oven and give the vegetables a stir. Melt the butter over the chicken skin and return the casserole dish to the oven, uncovered, for another 20 minutes to crisp up the skin.

4. Check to see if the chicken is done – the juices should run clear from the thickest part of the thigh when pierced with a skewer. If the chicken isn't quite ready, put it back in the oven for another 5–10 minutes.

5. When the chicken is cooked, put it on a serving platter and keep it warm. Arrange the vegetables around the chicken. Squash the flesh from the garlic cloves and add it all to the liquid in the dish. Put the dish over the heat and simmer until the liquid has reduced down a little to make a thin gravy. Pour the gravy into a warm jug and serve it with the chicken and vegetables and perhaps some greens on the side.

Chicken Fried Rice

If you have any leftover chicken from your pot roast (page 130) this is the perfect way to use it up. And it's super fast – just chop, chop, stir, stir and it's on the plate. You can buy cooked brown rice for recipes like this but it's cheaper to cook your own. A great time-saving tip is to have some basic carbs, such as cooked brown rice, in the freezer. It comes in useful for so many dishes or just as a side for those who want something extra.

Serves 4

bunch of spring onions,
    sliced into rounds

3 garlic cloves,
    finely sliced

30g fresh root ginger,
    finely sliced

500g cooked brown rice

about 200g cooked
    chicken, diced

200g peas, defrosted
    if frozen

1 tsp Chinese five-spice
    powder

2 tbsp soy sauce

2 eggs

a few coriander leaves,
    to garnish (optional)

1. Heat a tablespoon of vegetable oil in a wok. When it's very hot – the air above the wok should be shimmering – add the spring onions, garlic and ginger. Fry for a couple of minutes, then add the rice, chicken and peas.

2. Continue to fry for a couple of minutes, then sprinkle in the Chinese five-spice and the soy sauce. Taste for seasoning and add a little more soy sauce or some salt if necessary.

3. Beat the eggs together in a bowl and season them with salt and pepper. Push the contents of the wok to one side. Hold the wok at an angle so your burner is under the exposed part of the wok including part of the side, then add the eggs. Stir so they cook very quickly. When they are set, break them up and fold everything together.

4. Serve immediately, garnished with some coriander if you like.

Chicken Soup

If you've cooked the pot-roast chicken on page 130, don't chuck the carcass out. Use it to make stock for this beautiful chicken soup. Add any scraps of leftover meat and you'll be getting every bit of goodness from your bird.

Serves 4

15g butter

2 leeks, finely sliced

4 salad potatoes, sliced

3 garlic cloves, finely chopped

zest and juice of 1 lemon

2 large sprigs of tarragon, finely chopped, some reserved to garnish

750ml chicken stock (see p.199)

1 large courgette, thinly sliced

150g cooked chicken, diced

150ml single cream

1. Heat the butter in a large saucepan and add the leeks and potatoes. Season with salt and pepper and add a splash of water. Cover the pan and braise the vegetables gently until they are almost cooked through – this will take about 10 minutes.

2. Add the garlic cloves, lemon zest and tarragon, reserving some for garnishing the soup, then pour in the chicken stock. Bring to the boil and simmer for 5 minutes, then add the courgette and cook for another 5 minutes.

3. Add the diced chicken and cream and warm through gently without letting the soup boil. Add half the lemon juice and taste for seasoning, then add more lemon juice if you think the soup needs it.

4. Serve with some of the reserved tarragon sprinkled over each bowlful.

Lamb Keema Peas

This is another great recipe for time-saving batch cooking. Just double the quantities and portion it up to put in the freezer – lovely to have some meals all ready for those nights when you're really under pressure. I've suggested fresh mince here but you could also use finely chopped roast lamb.

Serves 4

500g lean lamb mince

1 onion, finely chopped

1 red pepper, finely chopped

1 courgette, roughly grated

30g fresh root ginger, finely chopped

small bunch of coriander, stems and leaves separated, both finely chopped

3 garlic cloves, finely chopped

1 tbsp mild curry powder (shopbought or see p.194)

1 sweet potato, peeled and diced

300g peas (or a mixture of peas and broad beans)

1. Heat a tablespoon of olive oil in a large saucepan. Add the lamb and cook it over a high heat until well browned, stirring regularly. If you find the lamb has given out a lot of fat, strain some off with a spoon, then add the onion and red pepper.

2. Turn the heat down and gently cook the onion and pepper for several minutes until they start to soften, then stir in the courgette, ginger, coriander stems, garlic, curry powder and sweet potato. Stir for another 3–4 minutes over a medium heat then pour in 300ml of water. Season with salt and pepper.

3. Bring to the boil, then turn the heat down and cover the pan. Cook for 20 minutes, then add the peas. Simmer for another 20 minutes until the peas are very soft and tender.

4. Sprinkle with the coriander leaves and serve with some brown rice or wholemeal pitta or naan bread if you like.

DAVINA'S TIP: *For extra flavour use 300ml of chicken or vegetable stock instead of water.*

Life is busy, busy, busy these days and sometimes it's nice just to let yourself slow down for a while. The recipes in this chapter all take a little longer than those in the rest of the book, but that doesn't necessarily mean they are a lot of work. Some, such as the Mediterranean chicken skewers and the salmon, simply need time to marinate. Others can be left bubbling gently on the stove for an hour or two or baking in the oven while you get on with other things. The gnocchi and the lasagne do need a quite a bit of prep but they're well worth it. Just put on some tyooooons and enjoy a bit of cooking therapy.

Slow
Down

Pumpkin Gnocchi with Spinach

This is totally delicious. Yes, it does take a bit of work so it's one for the weekend and perhaps for a time when you have a few helping hands around to shape the gnocchi? I find it really therapeutic.

Serves 4

100g pumpkin purée (from a can)

100g ricotta

150g wholemeal flour, plus extra for dusting

25g Parmesan cheese, grated, plus extra to serve

1 egg

75g pancetta or streaky bacon, diced

½ tsp sage

1 garlic clove, finely chopped

15g butter (optional)

250g spinach

1. If the pumpkin purée is quite wet, drain it in a colander lined with kitchen paper for a few minutes. Tip it into a bowl with the ricotta. Whizz the flour in a food processor until it's very fine, then add it to the pumpkin and ricotta. Add the Parmesan and egg, then season well and mix everything together. The dough will be soft but shouldn't be too sticky. Add a little more flour if it is sticky, but try not to add too much. Don't overwork the mixture or the gnocchi will be tough.

2. Turn the dough out on to a lightly floured surface. Divide it into 6 pieces, then roll each piece out into a sausage shape about the thickness of chipolatas. Cut these into lengths of about 1.5cm. You can leave them like this or mark them by lightly pressing a fork into the back of them.

3. Bring a large pan of water to the boil and add salt. Add the gnocchi a few at a time. They will sink to the bottom of the pan. When they have floated to the top, count slowly to ten, by which time they should be done. Scoop them out, then continue until you have cooked them all.

4. To serve, heat 2 tablespoons of olive oil in a large frying pan. Add the pancetta or bacon and cook until it starts to crisp up. Add the sage, garlic and gnocchi and continue to cook until the gnocchi take on some colour, shaking the pan regularly. Add the butter, if using.

5. Meanwhile, wash the spinach well and put it into a large pan over a gentle heat. When it has just wilted down (not collapsed completely), drain it and add it to the gnocchi. Season with salt and pepper and serve immediately with some extra grated Parmesan if you like.

Spinach and Ricotta Lasagne

Lasagne makes such a great one-pot supper – something you can bring to the table, serve up and keep everyone happy. My friends purr with pleasure when they see this. You do need to make the delish tomato sauce but if you have a batch ready in the freezer you can put this together in no time. If you're making this for vegetarians, check that all the cheese you're using is suitable.

Serves 6

500g spinach, washed
250g ricotta
50g vegetarian Parmesan-
    style cheese, finely
    grated
grating of nutmeg
1 litre tomato sauce
    (see p.123)
9 sheets of wholemeal or
    green lasagne
small bunch of basil leaves
2 x 125g mozzarella balls

1. Preheat the oven to 200°C/Fan 180°C/Gas 6.

2. Put the spinach in a large saucepan and cook it until it has completely collapsed. You won't need to add any extra water to it if it is still wet from washing. Drain the spinach well and when it is cool enough to handle, squeeze out as much of the excess liquid as you can, then chop it finely.

3. Put the spinach in a bowl and add the ricotta, half the grated cheese and a good grating of nutmeg, then season well with salt and pepper. Divide the mixture into 3 portions.

4. To assemble the lasagne, spread a quarter of the tomato sauce over the base of an ovenproof dish and top with 3 sheets of lasagne. Take a portion of spinach and ricotta and dot teaspoonfuls all over the lasagne sheets. Add a few basil leaves, then cover with the next quarter of tomato sauce and top with another 3 lasagne sheets. Repeat, adding another layer of spinach and ricotta, basil leaves, tomato sauce and lasagne. Spread the remaining tomato sauce on top, followed by more basil, then dot the last of the ricotta and spinach and basil leaves on top. Break up the mozzarella balls and arrange the pieces around the ricotta so all the sauce is covered. Sprinkle over the remaining grated cheese.

5. Bake the lasagne in the preheated oven for 30 minutes until the pasta has softened and the top is well browned and bubbling.

Mushroom Cobbler

A cobbler is a fab baked dish with a scone-like topping. I've eaten sweet ones before but this is a sensational savoury version. Nothing complicated and you can get the filling ready in advance, then make the topping just before popping the cobbler in the oven. And did you know that mushrooms are tipped to be the next superfood?!

Serves 4

65g butter

3 leeks, thickly sliced

750g mushrooms (mixture of portobellini, chestnut and large white), sliced

2 garlic cloves, finely chopped

2 sprigs of thyme

1 tbsp tomato purée

150ml red wine

150ml vegetable stock

200g wholemeal self-raising flour

1 egg

125ml buttermilk

1. Heat 15g of the butter with a tablespoon of olive oil in a large saucepan, then add the leeks. Cover the pan and cook the leeks over a medium heat until tender, then transfer them to a plate with a slotted spoon.

2. Turn up the heat and add the mushrooms to the pan. Cook them quickly until they're lightly browned and any liquid they have given out has evaporated. Add the garlic and cook for a further 2 minutes, then add the thyme and the tomato purée and stir to combine.

3. Pour over the wine, bring to the boil and allow it to bubble for a couple of minutes, then add the stock. Season with plenty of salt and pepper and put the leeks back in the pan. Simmer for 10 minutes.

4. To make the topping, put the flour into a bowl and add a generous pinch of salt. Add the remaining 50g of butter and rub it in with your fingertips. Mix the egg with the buttermilk, add this to the flour and butter, then mix to form a sticky dough.

5. Preheat the oven to 200°C/Fan 180°C/Gas 6. To assemble, put the filling in a deep ovenproof dish. Drop tablespoons of the cobbler topping over the filling, spacing them out well as they will spread while they cook. Bake the cobbler in the oven for about 30 minutes until the topping is well risen and a golden brown.

DAVINA'S TIP: *For extra flavour, sprinkle about 50g of grated vegetarian Cheddar over the cobbler before putting it in the oven. This adds about 50 calories to each serving.*

Slow-braised Squid

I'm seeing more and more squid in the supermarkets and fishmongers and it's usually reasonably priced. It can be cooked very quickly but I like this braised dish in which the squid and vegetables are cooked long and slow until they're beautifully tender. Very easy.

Serves 4

600g squid, sliced into rings (easiest to buy the tubes)

1 large fennel bulb, thinly sliced, any fronds reserved

2 garlic cloves, finely chopped

250ml white wine

600g salad potatoes, sliced if large

200g fresh ripe tomatoes, peeled and chopped

1 sprig of fresh thyme

small bunch of parsley, finely chopped

1. Wash the squid well, then dry it thoroughly with kitchen paper and season with salt. Heat a tablespoon of olive oil in a large pan. When the oil is very hot, add the squid and cook it very quickly until it's lightly coloured. Remove it from the pan and set it aside on a plate.

2. Heat another tablespoon of oil in the pan and add the fennel. Cook it over a high heat for at least 5 minutes until it starts to take on some colour, then add the garlic. Cook for another minute, then tip the squid back into the dish. Pour in the wine and allow it to bubble up for a couple of minutes, then add 150ml of water.

3. Season with salt and pepper and bring the liquid to the boil. Turn down the heat and cover the pan. Leave the squid and fennel to simmer for 45 minutes, then add the potatoes and continue to cook for a further 15 minutes.

4. Add the tomatoes and thyme and cook until the squid, fennel and potatoes are completely tender and the tomatoes have broken down. Serve garnished with finely chopped parsley.

Marinated Salmon with Brown Rice

We all know we should be eating oily fish, such as salmon, and this is just the easiest way to cook it. You do need to allow it to marinate, though, so this is a good recipe for the weekend or when you have a little more time. I love to serve this with the mint and yoghurt sauce on page 193. BTW, remember that almonds are really good for you – they're not just decoration here.

Serves 4

4 x 150g skinless salmon fillets
250g plain yoghurt
4 garlic cloves, crushed
30g fresh root ginger, grated
1 tbsp mild curry powder
1 tsp chilli powder (optional)
juice of 1 lemon
small bunch of coriander, a few leaves reserved to garnish
200g brown basmati rice
25g almonds

1. Season the salmon lightly with salt. Put the yoghurt in a food processor with the garlic, ginger, curry powder, chilli powder, if using, lemon juice and most of the coriander – save some leaves to use as a garnish. Blitz to make a vibrant green marinade, then tip this into a bowl and add the salmon. Cover and leave the fish to marinate for at least an hour or overnight – no longer.

2. Cook the rice according to the instructions on the packet. Lightly toast the almonds in a dry frying pan.

3. To cook the salmon, preheat the oven to 200°C/Fan 180°C/Gas 6. Scrape off any excess marinade from the salmon and arrange the pieces in a roasting tin, making sure they have plenty of space around them. Bake for about 12 minutes until just cooked through.

4. Serve the salmon and brown rice garnished with almonds and coriander and some mint and yoghurt sauce (see p.193) on the side.

Mediterranean Chicken Skewers

Very little work involved in this but you do need to allow some time for the marinade to work its magic. I love to serve these skewers with the Mediterranean vegetables on page 153 to make a meal that feels like a summer holiday. The mint and yoghurt sauce on page 193 is good with this too.

Serves 4

zest and juice of 1 lemon

1 tsp dried oregano

½ tsp dried thyme

½ tsp dried rosemary

2 garlic cloves, crushed

6 boneless, skinless chicken thighs OR 4 breast fillets, diced

1 red onion, cut into wedges

1 green pepper, cut into chunks

lemon wedges, to serve

1. Put the lemon zest and juice, herbs and garlic into a bowl that's large enough to hold the chicken and stir in 2 tablespoons of olive oil. Season the chicken with salt and pepper and add it to the marinade. Turn the chicken so it's all coated in the marinade, then cover the bowl with cling film and leave it in the fridge for at least 3 hours or overnight – no longer.

2. An hour before you're ready to cook the chicken, remove it from the fridge and allow it to come up to room temperature. Preheat the oven to 220°C/Fan 200°C/Gas 7.

3. Thread the pieces of chicken on to 8 skewers, interspersing them with wedges of onion and pepper, then put the skewers on a baking tray. Brush the onion and pepper with any remaining marinade.

4. Bake the chicken skewers in the oven for 20 minutes until lightly charred and cooked through, turning them over once or twice, Alternatively, cook them on a barbecue or a griddle. Serve the chicken skewers with lemon wedges to squeeze over them.

Mediterranean Vegetables

This is such an easy way of serving up loads of my favourite veggies. Although it doesn't take long to put together it does take a while to cook, but once it's in the oven you can forget about it. Perfect with the chicken skewers on page 151 or as a vegetarian dish with salad and perhaps some couscous.

Serves 4

600g floury potatoes, thickly sliced

1 large aubergine, halved lengthways and sliced

2 red onions, cut into wedges

2 peppers (any colour or a mixture), deseeded and thickly sliced

2 large courgettes, sliced into rounds

600g tomatoes, peeled, deseeded and chopped

3 garlic cloves, finely chopped

1 tsp dried oregano

2 tbsp red wine vinegar

small bunch of basil leaves, to garnish

1. Preheat the oven to 200°C/Fan 180°C/Gas 6. Put the potatoes, aubergine, red onions, peppers and courgettes in a large ovenproof dish or a roasting tin.

2. Add the tomatoes and mix thoroughly, then sprinkle over the garlic and oregano. Drizzle over 2 tablespoons of olive oil. Cover the dish with foil and bake the vegetables for 1 hour.

3. Mix the red wine vinegar with 100ml of water. Remove the dish of vegetables from the oven, take off the foil and pour over the vinegar and water mixture – don't stir or you might break up the vegetables.

4. Put the dish back in the oven, uncovered, for another 30 minutes until everything is tender and starting to brown lightly. Garnish with the basil leaves and serve hot or at room temperature.

Chicken Meatballs with Couscous and Creamy Tomato Sauce

Using some couscous in these meatballs makes them lovely and light – and you can serve the rest of the couscous alongside. I'm loving the orange and lemon flavour in the couscous too. There's a bit of work but it's kind of soothing and if you have some tomato sauce ready in the fridge or freezer the whole thing doesn't take too long. And when you taste it – mmmmm, it's well worth the time.

Serves 4

150g wholemeal couscous

2 tsp cinnamon

zest of 2 lemons

juice of 2 oranges

500g chicken mince

1 onion, very finely
  chopped

small bunches of parsley,
  mint and dill, finely
  chopped

1 egg

500ml tomato sauce
  (see p.123)

100ml double cream

1. First prepare the couscous. Put the couscous in a bowl with plenty of salt and pepper, a teaspoon of the cinnamon and the zest of one of the lemons. Add 100ml of hot water and the juice of one of the oranges. Leave the couscous to stand until all the water and juice has been absorbed, then fluff it up with a fork.

2. Preheat the oven to 200°C/Fan 180°C/Gas 6. Put the chicken in a bowl and add 75g of the prepared couscous. Heat a tablespoon of olive oil in a frying pan, add the onion and fry gently until it is very soft and translucent. Remove the pan from the heat and leave the onion to cool.

3. Add the cooled onion to the chicken mince with half the herbs, the remaining lemon zest and the egg. Stir thoroughly to combine, then form the mixture into 16 balls. Place them on a large baking tray and bake them in the oven for 18–20 minutes.

4. When the meatballs are nearly ready, put the tomato sauce in a small saucepan with the remaining cinnamon and orange juice. Bring it to the boil and simmer for 5 minutes. Check for seasoning and then stir in the cream. Heat the sauce through, making sure you don't let it boil.

5. Stir most of the remaining herbs into the couscous, reserving a couple of tablespoons for the garnish. Remove the meatballs from the oven and serve them with couscous and the sauce spooned over the top. Garnish with the remaining herbs.

Chicken Curry

I confess that I prefer mild curries to those that blow your socks off and this is a lovely gentle, pretty dish that includes some dried rose petals. I love it! You can buy edible rose petals in healthfood shops and online and they keep for ages.

Serves 4

8 skinless, boneless chicken thighs, cut into bite-sized pieces

1 tsp ground cardamom

1 tsp ground coriander

½ tsp fennel seeds

1 tbsp dried rose petals, plus extra to garnish

25g butter

1 onion, sliced

2 garlic cloves, crushed

20g fresh root ginger, grated

200g yoghurt

1. Put the chicken in a bowl and season it with salt and pepper (preferably white pepper). Put the cardamom, coriander, fennel seeds and the tablespoon of rose petals in a spice grinder and whizz to make a fine powder. Sprinkle this mixture over the chicken pieces and stir, then set the bowl aside.

2. Heat the butter in a large pan. Add the onion and cook it very gently until it's soft and translucent. Add the garlic and ginger, then continue to cook for 2–3 minutes.

3. Add the chicken to the pan and cook it over a medium heat until lightly coloured on all sides. Pour over 300ml of water and bring it to the boil. Then turn the heat down and simmer for 20–25 minutes until the chicken is completely cooked through and the liquid has reduced. Stir in the yoghurt and simmer for a few minutes more, making sure it doesn't boil – you don't want the sauce to separate.

4. Garnish with extra rose petals and serve with some brown rice or some Indian bread.

   DAVINA'S TIP: *Water is fine for this but it's even better made with good chicken stock – see my recipe on p.199. For extra heat and flavour, add some finely sliced chillies and a few mint leaves just before serving.*

Sausage Casserole

A blissfully easy supper, this doesn't take long to put together and you can leave it simmering happily while you get on with something else. Sausages and beans are a classic combination that everyone loves but if you want a lower-cal meal, leave out the beans and the dish will still be yummy.

Serves 4

8 pork sausages

1 onion, thickly sliced

2 carrots, thickly sliced on the diagonal

200g celeriac, diced

2 garlic cloves, finely chopped

1 tsp dried thyme

250ml red wine

200ml chicken or beef stock

400g can of tomatoes

400g can of cannellini beans, drained (optional)

1. Heat a teaspoon of olive oil in a frying pan. Add the sausages and fry them over a fairly high heat until well browned all over. Remove the pan from the heat.

2. Heat 2 teaspoons of olive oil in a large pan. Add the onion, carrots and celeriac and fry them gently until they're starting to caramelise and soften around the edges. Add the garlic and thyme to the pan and season well with salt and pepper, then add the browned sausages and cover with the red wine. Bring to the boil and simmer until the red wine has reduced down by about a third.

3. Add the stock, cover the pan and continue to simmer for 10 minutes. Pour in the tomatoes and add the beans, if using. Simmer for another half an hour, by which time the sausages and vegetables will be perfectly tender. Serve with some green veg on the side.

Marinated Lamb with Cauliflower Couscous

This is another dish that's quick to prep and cook but does need time to marinate in order to taste its best. I love lamb but it is quite high in calories so it's good to serve it with this low-cal but totally lovely cauli couscous. Ras-el-hanout is a North African spice mix and you can buy it in supermarkets.

Serves 4

8 small lamb chops or
   4 lamb steaks

1 tbsp Moroccan spice mix
   (see p.194) OR 1 tbsp
   ras-el-hanout

juice of ½ lemon

4 garlic cloves, crushed
   or grated

lemon wedges, to serve

Cauliflower couscous

1 small cauliflower,
   broken into florets

2 oranges

small bunches of mint and
   parsley, finely chopped

½ cucumber, finely diced

1 small red onion, very
   finely diced

1. Put the lamb chops or steaks in a dish and season them with salt and pepper. Mix the spice mix or ras-el-hanout with the lemon juice, garlic and 4 tablespoons of olive oil. Pour the mixture over the lamb and massage it into the meat. Cover the dish and leave the meat to marinate in the fridge for at least an hour or overnight.

2. For the couscous, blitz the cauliflower in a food processor until it resembles breadcrumbs. Cut a small slice off the top and bottom of one of the oranges and sit it on your work surface. Cut away the skin and membrane, following the contour of the orange. Dice the orange flesh, removing any pips and any large pieces of membrane. Pour any juices into a jug or bowl and squeeze out any juice from the membrane. Repeat with the other orange.

3. Heat 2 tablespoons of oil in a large frying pan. Add the cauliflower and stir it for a minute or so, then add about 100ml of water. Cook over a medium heat for about 5 minutes until the water has evaporated and the cauliflower is dry and opaque looking, with the raw edge taken off, Tip the cauliflower into a bowl. When it has cooled down, add the orange flesh and juice, herbs, cucumber and red onion. Mix thoroughly.

4. Remove the lamb from the fridge an hour before you want to cook it. Heat a griddle pan (or prepare a barbecue) until very hot. Grill the chops or steaks for 3–4 minutes on each side until just pink in the middle. Leave them to rest for at least 5 minutes before serving with the cauliflower couscous and lemon wedges.

Mediterranean Shoulder of Lamb

What I like on a Sunday is to have something cooking gently in the oven and smelling wonderful while I get on with other things. This dish is perfect. It needs very little attention and it tastes incredible. If you do have any leftover meat, use it to make the keema peas on page 136.

Serves 6

2kg shoulder of lamb, on the bone

cloves from 1 bulb of garlic, peeled and cut into thin slices

2 large sprigs of rosemary, broken up into spikes

1 onion, finely chopped

3 x 400g cans of flageolet beans, drained

300ml vegetable stock

4 fresh tomatoes, peeled and diced

small bunch of parsley, chopped, to garnish

1. Preheat the oven to its highest setting. Take the shoulder of lamb and cut deep slits at regular intervals all over the skin and any exposed flesh. Stuff the thin slivers of garlic and rosemary spikes into the cuts. Rub the lamb all over with a tablespoon of olive oil, then season it well with salt and pepper.

2. Place the lamb in a large roasting tin and cover it with foil. Put it in the oven and immediately turn the temperature down to 170°C/Fan 150°C/Gas 3–4. Leave the lamb to cook for up to 4 hours, checking after 3 hours – it will be done when the meat is falling off the bone and can easily be pulled apart.

3. Put the lamb on a warmed serving platter and leave it to rest. Drain off any liquid from the roasting tin into a jug and wait for it to settle, then skim off any fat. Transfer the skimmed juices to a small saucepan and heat them through.

4. Heat a tablespoon of olive oil in a large saucepan. Add the onion and cook it gently until soft and translucent. Add the beans, stock and tomatoes and season with salt and pepper. Bring to the boil, then turn down the heat and leave to simmer until the tomatoes have broken down and the beans are piping hot.

5. Serve the lamb with the strained pan juices and the beans, garnished with parsley.

I've always had a seriously sweet tooth and I'm proud to say that I've really got it under control these days. I'm no longer like a crazy thing hunting down the children's left-over treats, and I look and feel much better. Added sugar is just not good for us or our blood sugar levels. But I do like the odd sweet something from time to time so I cook puddings and bakes *without* any table sugar. I prefer to rely on the natural sweetness of fruit and vegetables with the occasional touch of maple syrup or honey. Try my banana and peanut butter ice cream, sugar-free crumble or pear and blueberry galette and you'll never yearn for sugary puddings again.

Puddings and Bakes

Spiced Banana Bread

This is just the thing to have around when anyone fancies a little something in the afternoon - as members of my family often do! It's good on its own or extra yummy spread with butter and I really like it toasted. Just make sure you get soft figs or dates so they purée easily.

Makes 12 slices

225g wholemeal flour
(wheat or spelt)
1 heaped tbsp baking
powder
2 tsp cinnamon
½ tsp grated nutmeg
150g soft dried figs OR
pitted dates
300ml buttermilk
4 eggs
3 very ripe bananas,
mashed

1. Preheat the oven to 180°C/Fan 160°C/Gas 4. Line a large loaf tin with baking paper.

2. Put the flour, baking powder and spices into a large bowl with a generous pinch of salt and whisk together.

3. Snip the tough stems off the figs. Cut the figs, or dates, into small pieces, then put them in a food processor or blender with the buttermilk and eggs. Whizz together until well combined – the buttermilk should turn the colour of honey. Stir in the bananas.

4. Pour the combined wet ingredients into the dry ingredients and mix together, trying to keep stirring to a minimum. Pour the mixture into the prepared loaf tin.

5. Bake the banana bread for about an hour until it is well risen, rich golden brown in colour and a skewer comes out clean. Check it at regular intervals and if the top is getting too dark, cover it with a sheet of foil.

6. Leave the banana bread to cool in the tin for 10 minutes, then turn it out on to a cooling rack. Cut it into thick slices.

Peaches and Raspberries

I love warm peaches and this is a super-quick sweet treat for the summer months when these fruits are at their best. It shouldn't need any extra sweetness but if you find your fruit is on the sharp side you could add a little drizzle of honey if you fancy. Peachy!

Serves 4

4 ripe but firm peaches
15g butter, melted
200g raspberries
100–125ml crème fraiche
15g flaked almonds
drizzle of honey (optional)

1. Heat a griddle pan to medium – you don't want it too hot or the peaches will burn on the cut side before they have softened slightly. Cut the peaches in half and remove the stones.

2. Brush the cut side of each peach half with butter, then place them cut-side down on the griddle. Grill the peaches for 5 minutes, or until they lift off the griddle with ease and have definite char markings. Flip them over and cook skin-side down for another 5 minutes. Brush the cut side with butter again, then flip them over and cook them cut-side down for another 4–5 minutes. The peaches may be slightly firm in the middle but that's fine.

3. Remove the skins if you like – they should slip off very easily – then divide the peaches between 4 bowls or glasses.

4. Top the peaches with the raspberries and crème fraiche. Toast the almonds in a dry frying pan, until very lightly coloured and sprinkle some over each serving. Add a drizzle of honey if you want a little extra sweetness. Serve immediately.

Banana and Peanut Butter Ice Cream

This is the easiest ice cream you can imagine – you just whizz up frozen bananas with nut butter and a hint of lime and you have something totally divine. It's excellent just on its own but if you really want to go mad, try this dark choc sauce. Just an occasional treat, mind!

Serves 4

4 large, ripe bananas
(not black)

2 tbsp nut butter (peanut
or any other kind)

zest of 1 lime

½ tsp cinnamon (optional)

**Chocolate sauce
(optional)**

50g dark chocolate
(100% cocoa solids)

50g maple syrup

150ml single cream

 (ice cream only)

1. Line a large baking tray with baking paper. Peel the bananas and slice them into rounds. Place them in a single layer on the baking paper, then freeze them for 2 hours.

2. Put the frozen bananas in a blender or food processor. Blitz, scraping down the sides of the jug or bowl regularly, until the bananas have broken down and have a smooth and creamy texture.

3. Add the peanut butter, lime zest and cinnamon, if using, and process again until everything is well combined. The mixture will have the consistency of soft ice cream. If you want to firm it up a little, you can transfer it to the freezer for another hour or so. Serve with or without chocolate sauce.

4. To make the chocolate sauce, break up the chocolate and put it in a saucepan with the maple syrup, single cream and a pinch of salt. Stir over a very gentle heat until everything has melted together and you have a smooth, liquid sauce. Serve hot or cold – the sauce will firm up a little as it cools.

Watermelon, Clementine and Strawberry Granita

Best to try this one at a weekend or on a day when you're around in the kitchen so you can keep checking on its progress in the freezer and breaking up the crystals – kids love to help with this. These three fruits make a magic combination and this is a stunning low-calorie pudding.

Serves 4

300g ripe watermelon, cut into chunks
2 clementines, peeled, any seeds removed
juice of 1 lime
150g strawberries, hulled
25g honey (optional)

 (without honey)

1. Put all the ingredients, including the honey, if using, into a blender. Blitz to make as smooth a mixture as you can.

2. Push the mixture through a sieve, then transfer it to a shallow container and put it in the freezer. Freeze for about 45 minutes, by which time the mixture will have started to freeze around the edges. Take the container out, break the crystals up with a fork and mix them into the unfrozen liquid, then put it back in the freezer.

3. Keep checking and breaking up the ice crystals every 30–45 minutes until everything is frozen. Serve in small glasses

4. Alternatively, you can freeze the mixture until solid, then transfer it to a blender and blitz to a slush.

Frozen Fruit

This sounds like the easiest thing in the world but only if you know which fruits to use. Some, such as melons and pears, freeze too hard and aren't pleasant to bite into while others turn to mush too quickly when they come out of the freezer. Others lose sweetness so don't taste so good. The following all freeze well and are at their best when frozen for up to two hours.

Serves 4

1 mango, peeled and cut
  into slices
1 papaya, peeled, deseeded
  and cut into pieces
¼ small watermelon,
  peeled and cut into
  triangles
juice of 2 limes
bunch of green or purple
  seedless grapes
handful of blueberries

1. Line a baking tray with baking paper. Put the mango, papaya and watermelon pieces in a bowl with the lime juice and toss well.

2. Tip the fruit on the baking tray and add the grapes and blueberries. Put the tray in the freezer and open freeze the fruit for 1½–2 hours. You can eat the fruit immediately – the texture will be just right, as you will be able to bite through it comfortably.

3. Alternatively, decant the frozen fruit into a bag and keep it in the freezer for an instant snack. Once you take the fruit out of the freezer, eat it soon, as the texture will disintegrate quickly when it starts defrosting.

DAVINA'S TIP: *Be sure to use seedless grapes – it's really hard to remove seeds from a frozen grape!*

Fig Rolls

These are my version of a very traditional biscuit and I have to say they're good. No added sugar either, as all the sweetness comes from the fruit. The pastry is quite crumbly but handle it gently and you'll be fine. Perfect for when you have a moment of peace with a cup of coffee.

Makes 16

175g wholemeal flour
(wheat or spelt)
50g ground almonds
½ tsp baking powder
125g butter, chilled
and cubed
1 egg yolk
2–4 tbsp milk

Filling

300g soft dried figs,
hard tips snipped off
juice of 1 orange and
½ tsp orange zest

1. First make the pastry. Put the flour, ground almonds and baking powder into a bowl with a pinch of salt. Add the butter and rub it in with your fingertips until you have a mixture that resembles fine breadcrumbs. Add the egg yolk and the milk, a tablespoon at a time, mixing until a soft dough forms. Make sure the dough isn't too crumbly and if it is, add a little more milk. Form the dough into a ball and wrap it in cling film. Chill it in the fridge for up to an hour.

2. Roughly chop the figs and put them in a saucepan with the orange juice and zest and a pinch of salt. Add 150ml of water. Simmer until the figs start to break down and just about all of the liquid has evaporated – this will take 15–20 minutes. Keep stirring regularly. Remove the pan from the heat and cool down, then blitz the figs to a paste in a food processor. Chill for half an hour.

3. Preheat the oven to 180°C/Fan 160°C/Gas 4. Roll out the dough into a large rectangle about 32 x 20cm. Cut the dough in half lengthways, so you have 2 long strips. Divide the fig filling in half, and spread it in a long sausage shape down the centre of each strip of dough, leaving a border on each side. Moisten the uncovered edges with a little water, then bring them together over the filling, sealing them as you go. Roll over and carefully smooth over any cracks with a knife.

4. Cut each strip of dough into 8 pieces, about 4cm long, and arrange them on a baking tray. Mark lines across each fig roll with a fork if you like. Bake for 20–25 minutes until the pastry is completely cooked through and a lightly speckled golden brown. Remove the fig rolls from the oven and put them on a wire rack to cool. Store in an airtight container.

Chocolate and Coconut Biscuits

I have to confess that I have a weakness for the occasional biscuit and these are so easy to make. Yes, they do contain butter and quite a lot of maple syrup but if you just have one at a time they shouldn't break your calorie budget.

Makes 30

200g butter
175g maple syrup
250g wholemeal flour,
    preferably spelt
50g cocoa powder
300g desiccated coconut
2 tsp baking powder
25g dark chocolate
    (100% cocoa solids),
    coarsely grated

1. Melt the butter in a small pan and pour it into a bowl. Add the maple syrup and stir to combine. If the butter is still warm, leave it to cool until tepid.

2. Put the flour in a separate bowl with the cocoa powder, desiccated coconut, baking powder and a large pinch of salt. Add the butter and maple syrup mixture to the dry ingredients along with the chocolate and mix well to make a dough. Wrap the dough in cling film and put it in the fridge to chill for half an hour.

3. Preheat the oven to 200°C/Fan 180°C/Gas 6. Line 2 baking trays with non-stick baking paper.

4. Divide the mixture into 30 equal-sized balls. Squash each ball into a 6.5cm cookie cutter and place the biscuits on the baking trays. Bake them for 18–20 minutes until they start to crisp round the edges – you can't really tell by colour because of the cocoa. Transfer them to a wire rack to cool.

Apple and Carrot Steamed Puddings

Love, love, love these. There's only a small amount of maple syrup as most of the sweetness comes from the apple and carrot. Who would have thought a steamed pudding could be so low in calories? These are light and luscious – a real treat. They're best eaten hot or while still warm.

Serves 6

75g raisins
150g wholemeal flour
2 tsp baking powder
½ tsp bicarbonate of soda
1 tbsp ground ginger
2 tsp cinnamon
75ml buttermilk
25ml maple syrup
2 eggs
1 eating apple, peeled and finely grated
150g carrot (or sweet potato), finely grated

1. Grease 6 pudding basins with a little oil. Put the raisins in a bowl and cover them with just-boiled water. Leave them to stand while you make the sponge mixture.

2. Put the flour, baking powder, bicarbonate of soda and ginger into bowl and mix to combine. Add all the remaining ingredients and fold everything together until you have a soft batter with a dropping consistency. Drain the raisins and add them to the bowl at this point.

3. Divide the mixture between the pudding basins. Cover each basin with a piece of foil or baking paper, making sure you fold a pleat into the middle. Secure with string.

4. Put the puddings in a steamer over a saucepan or stand them on a trivet or a folded tea towel in the saucepan. Add just-boiled water to the lower part of the steamer or to come halfway up the sides of the puddings if they are in a saucepan. Steam for 45 minutes until well risen and springy to touch, checking that the water doesn't boil dry. Turn out and serve with single cream and a touch of maple syrup if you like.

DAVINA'S TIP: *It's important to grate the apple and carrot really finely for the best-textured puddings. Grate the apple over a bowl to catch any juice and add it to the mixture.*

Pear and Blueberry Galette

Galettes are like a sort of open fruit pie and are very easy to make as it doesn't matter if they don't look neat. The more rustic the better! Pears and blueberries make a tasty – and pretty – pud. If the pears are good and sweet you won't need the maple syrup.

Serves 6

3 ripe pears
juice and zest of ½ lime
½ tsp ground cardamom
100g blueberries
drizzle of maple syrup
    (optional)
25g butter

Pastry
250g wholemeal flour
    (wheat or spelt)
150g butter, chilled
    and cubed
1 egg yolk
beaten egg, for brushing

1. First make the pastry. Put the flour into a bowl with a pinch of salt. Add the butter and rub it in with your fingertips until the mixture resembles fine breadcrumbs. Add the egg yolk and just enough ice-cold water to bind the pastry into a smooth dough. Form it into a ball and make sure it isn't cracking, then wrap it in cling film and leave it to chill in the fridge for an hour.

2. Peel and core the pears, then cut them into thin wedges and put them in a bowl. Pour over the lime juice and toss to coat all the pieces of pear in the juice to stop them going brown. Sprinkle in the zest and the cardamom and add the blueberries, plus a little drizzle of maple syrup if you like.

3. Preheat the oven to 200°C/Fan 180°C/Gas 6. Roll the pastry out into a large round, then pile the pears and blueberries into the middle, leaving a border of about 5cm. Fold the pastry border over the fruit – much of the fruit will be left uncovered in the middle. Brush the edges of the pastry with beaten egg and dot pieces of butter over the top.

4. Transfer the galette to a baking tray and bake it in the oven for 35–40 minutes until well browned. Serve hot or cold with crème fraiche.

Blackberry and Apple Crumble

My family all love a crumble. Good old Kent Coxes apples work well for this as they soften nicely during the cooking – Granny Smiths aren't so good. It's up to you about the maple syrup in the filling, as it depends on the sweetness of your blackberries. Some can be quite tart.

Serves 6

1 large cooking apple and 4 eating apples, peeled and sliced
300g blackberries
1 tsp ground cinnamon
¼ tsp ground cloves
25ml maple syrup (optional)

Topping
150g wholemeal flour (wheat or spelt)
75g butter, diced
50g oats
25g hazelnuts, lightly crushed
25ml maple syrup

1. Preheat the oven to 180°C/Fan 160°C/Gas 4.

2. Put the apples and blackberries in a 1-litre ovenproof dish. Sprinkle over the cinnamon and cloves and mix thoroughly, then drizzle over the maple syrup, if using.

3. To make the topping, put the flour in a bowl with a pinch of salt. Add the butter and rub it in with your fingertips until the mixture is the texture of breadcrumbs. Stir in the oats and hazelnuts, then drizzle in the maple syrup. Mix again.

4. Spoon the crumble topping over the fruit. Bake the crumble in the preheated oven for 25–30 minutes until the topping is brown and the fruit is piping hot and bubbling up from underneath.

DAVINA'S TIP: *This is totally scrumptious just as it is, but sometimes I like to really spoil myself – and others – and I serve it with spoonfuls of crème fraiche.*

Pineapple and Grapefruit Salad with Coconut Cream

You do need to plan ahead to chill the coconut cream but once that's done this is a doddle and so totally tropically good. If the pineapple is really sweet you shouldn't need any maple syrup but see what you think.

Serves 4

400g can of coconut milk
1 ripe pineapple
2 grapefruit (white, red or pink)
a few sprigs of mint
1–2 tsp maple syrup, to taste (optional)

1. First make the coconut cream. Chill the can of coconut milk in the fridge, preferably overnight. Open it carefully and spoon off all the solid coconut cream which will have separated from the water. Put the coconut cream in a bowl and set the water aside to use another time. Whisk the coconut cream, preferably using electric beaters, until it forms soft peaks.

2. Cut the skin away from the pineapple and cut out the eyes – you will see you can follow a diagonal line when you cut them out rather than doing them individually. Cut the pineapple into thin rounds.

3. Cut a thin slice off the top and bottom of each grapefruit. Set one down on your work surface and following the contour of the fruit, cut away the skin and outer layer of membrane, working from top to bottom. Cut away any pith or membrane that remains. Slice the flesh into thin rounds, flicking out any seeds as you go. Repeat with the other grapefruit.

4. Arrange the slices of pineapple and grapefruit over a serving plate, then sprinkle with mint leaves. Drizzle with maple syrup, if using, and serve with the coconut cream.

Lime Sandwich Cake

Ahem – this is one for special occasions as it is quite calorific, but I think it is so good it's worth it. And you only need a small slice – good practice for your willpower! Spelt flour does work better than regular wholemeal here so do get hold of some if you can. Supermarkets sell it.

Makes 16 slices

225g butter, softened

zest of 2 limes and
juice of 1

225g wholemeal flour,
preferably spelt

2 heaped tsp baking
powder

3 eggs

225g maple syrup

Filling and topping

150g crème fraiche

50ml double cream

50ml cream cheese

zest and juice of 1 lime,
plus extra to garnish

1 tbsp maple syrup

1 mango, diced, plus
½ mango, thinly sliced,
to garnish

1. Preheat the oven to 180°C/Fan 160°C/Gas 4. Line 2 x 20cm sandwich tins with non-stick baking paper.

2. Beat the butter with the lime zest until very soft and well aerated – you can do this in a stand mixer or with a hand-held electric beater. Put the flour in a separate bowl and mix in a pinch of salt and the baking powder.

3. Add an egg to the butter along with a tablespoon of the flour mixture. Fold them in, then repeat until you have used up all 3 eggs. Fold in the remaining flour, followed by the maple syrup and the lime juice. The mixture should have a dropping consistency.

4. Divide the batter evenly between the 2 tins. Bake the cakes in the oven for about 20 minutes, until they are lightly golden brown, well risen, and shrinking away from the sides of the tins. Remove them from the oven and put them on a cooling rack. When the cakes are completely cool, take them out of the tins and peel off the baking paper.

5. Whisk together the crème fraiche, double cream, cream cheese, lime zest and juice and maple syrup. Set aside a third of this mixture for the top of the cake.

6. Mix the diced mango into the larger amount of cream mixture and spread it over the top of one of the cakes. Place the other cake on top. Pile the remaining cream mixture on top of the cake, forming a round in the centre, then arrange the mango slices on top. Garnish with a few strips of pared lime zest.

In this chapter you will find useful recipes for some kitchen basics, such as two kinds of pesto, home-made spice mixes and a few sauces. I've also included a veggie stock and chicken stock but don't feel the pressure to perform! You can buy good stocks now, and stock cubes with less salt added, but if you have time, home-made stock tastes really good and is a great way to use up a chicken carcass from your Sunday roast.

Basics

Pestos

Serves 6–8 (with pasta)

Classic green pesto

50g basil leaves

25g pine nuts

40g Parmesan, Pecorino
or Grana Padano
cheese (or vegetarian
equivalent), grated

1 garlic clove, crushed

zest of 1 lemon

Red pesto

1 tub of sunblush
tomatoes (about 240g)

25g pine nuts

10g basil leaves

10g parsley leaves

25g Parmesan, Pecorino
or Grana Padano
cheese (or vegetarian
equivalent), grated

1. For the green pesto, put the ingredients in a food processor with
2 tablespoons of olive oil and blitz to make a grainy paste. Taste
for seasoning and add salt and pepper as required, then mix again.

2. For the red pesto, put the ingredients in a food processor with
2 tablespoons of the oil from the tub of sunblush tomatoes and
blitz to make a grainy paste. Taste for seasoning and add salt
and pepper as required, then mix again.

3. Use right away or if you want to keep the pesto, add a layer of oil
on top to preserve the colour. The pestos will keep this way for up
to a week in the fridge.

Raw Tomato Salsa

Serves 4

4 ripe tomatoes, finely
chopped

½ red onion, finely
chopped

a few coriander leaves,
finely chopped

juice and zest of 1 lime

1. Put the tomatoes in a bowl with the red onion, coriander leaves and the lime juice and zest. Season well with salt and pepper, then drizzle over a tablespoon of olive oil. Leave the salsa to stand at room temperature for a while before serving so the flavours can blend.

Mint and Yoghurt Sauce

Serves 4

250g plain yoghurt

½ cucumber

2 tsp dried mint

1. Put the yoghurt in a bowl. Coarsely grate the cucumber and sprinkle it with salt. Leave it to drain in a colander for half an hour, then stir it into the yoghurt with the dried mint.

Mild Curry Powder

Makes 1 small jar

1 tbsp coriander seeds
2 tsp cumin seeds
1 tsp cardamom seeds
2cm cinnamon stick
½ tsp fenugreek seeds
½ tsp white peppercorns
½ tsp fennel seeds
½ tsp mustard seeds
2 cloves
1 tbsp ground turmeric

1. Put all the ingredients except the turmeric into a dry frying pan and toast them over a medium heat until you can smell the aroma of the spices and the mustard seeds have started to pop. Keep shaking the pan frequently.

2. Tip the seeds and spices out of the pan into a bowl and leave them to cool, then grind them in a spice grinder. Stir the turmeric into the mixture, then store the curry powder in an airtight jar until needed.

Moroccan Spice Mix

Makes 1 small jar

1 tbsp cumin seeds
1 tbsp coriander seeds
1 tsp black peppercorns
3cm cinnamon stick
½ tsp allspice berries
½ tsp cardamom seeds
2 cloves
2 tsp dried rose petals
   (optional)
1 tsp ground ginger
½–1 tsp cayenne pepper

1. Put the whole spices in a dry frying pan and toast them over a medium heat until you can smell their aroma. Keep shaking the pan frequently.

2. Tip the contents of the pan into a bowl and leave them to cool, then add the rose petals, if using, and grind everything in a spice grinder. Stir the ground ginger and cayenne to taste into the mixture, then store it in an airtight jar until needed.

Thai Curry Paste

Makes 1 small jar

2 shallots, peeled and chopped

4 garlic cloves, peeled and chopped

30g fresh root ginger, peeled and chopped

3 lemongrass stems, outer leaves peeled away, sliced

4 lime leaves, shredded

juice and finely grated zest of 2 limes

2–4 green chillies, to taste, sliced and deseeded if you like

large bunch of fresh coriander

1 tbsp ground coriander

1 tbsp ground cumin

1. Put all the ingredients in a food processor and season with plenty of salt and pepper.

2. Pulse, pushing the fresh coriander down at intervals, until everything is combined into a paste. It will not be completely smooth, but flecked with green from the coriander.

3. You can store this paste in the fridge for up to a week or divide it into portions and freeze.

Mayonnaise

Makes about 300ml

2 egg yolks
½ tsp Dijon mustard
300ml groundnut,
    sunflower or corn oil
squeeze of lemon juice

1. Put the egg yolks in a bowl and add a pinch of salt. Add the mustard and whisk briefly. Put the bowl on a folded tea towel on your work surface to stop it slipping around while you whisk. Start adding the oil a few drops at a time, whisking constantly until the egg yolks have completely absorbed the oil before adding more. Once you've added about a third of the oil, start adding a little more each time until it's a steady stream.

2. Once all the oil is incorporated, add a squeeze of lemon. Cover the bowl of mayo with cling film and keep it in the fridge.

3. If you like, you can make the mayonnaise in a food processor. Start by adding a few drops of oil at a time, then build up to a steady stream, as with the hand-whisking method.

39 calories per pepper • Prep: 5 minutes • Cooking: 30 minutes

Roasted Red Peppers

4 red peppers

1. Preheat the oven to 200°C/Fan 180°C/Gas 6. Cut the peppers in half lengthways and cut out the white membranes. Discard the stems and the seeds. Place the peppers in a roasting tin, cut side down, season with salt and pepper, then drizzle them with a tablespoon of olive oil.

2. Roast the peppers for 30 minutes or until the skins have started to blacken and blister. Remove the peppers from the oven and while they're still hot, put them into a plastic bag or a bowl with a lid. Leave them to steam until just warm. When the peppers are cool enough to handle, remove the skins – they should pull away easily. You can store these in the fridge for up to a week or freeze them for longer.

Corn Tortillas

Makes 12

250g golden tortilla flour
(masa harina)

1. Put the tortilla flour in a bowl and add 330ml of freshly boiled water. Mix thoroughly to bring the dough together, then knead the dough until it is smooth. If it feels too dry, wet your hands to work in more moisture. Divide the mixture into 12 pieces and roll each one into a ball.

2. Place a ball of dough between 2 pieces of cling film. Squash it flat with a tortilla press or using the base of a heavy-based saucepan or frying pan. If using a pan, make sure you place it so the dough is exactly in the centre – this will give you the best chance of getting a nice round. Alternatively, you can just roll the dough out. Repeat to make all the tortillas. Don't worry if your tortillas are slightly ragged around the edges – this adds to their charm. Set them aside.

3. To cook the tortillas, heat a heavy-based frying pan or griddle until it's very hot. Cook each tortilla for 15–20 seconds on the first side, until it will lift cleanly off, then flip and cook on the other side for 30 seconds. Flip again and cook on the first side for another 15 seconds. Keep the tortillas warm – wrap them in a tea towel on a plate or in a basket – while you cook the rest.

Vegetable Stock

Makes about 1.5 litres

2 large onions, roughly
  chopped
3 large carrots, chopped
4 celery sticks, sliced
1 leek, sliced
200g butternut squash,
  unpeeled, roughly
  chopped
100g button mushrooms,
  roughly chopped
large sprig of oregano
large sprig of parsley
1 bay leaf
a few peppercorns

1. Heat a tablespoon of olive oil in a large saucepan. Add all the vegetables and cook them over a high heat. Leave them for 5 minutes so they take on some colour on the underside, then stir. Continue to cook, stirring regularly until the vegetables are starting to caramelise.

2. Add the herbs and peppercorns to the saucepan, then pour over 2 litres of cold water. Bring the water to the boil, then turn the heat down to a gentle simmer. Leave the stock to simmer, uncovered, for an hour.

3. Strain the stock through a colander into a bowl, then strain it again through a sieve lined with either muslin or kitchen paper. This stock keeps well in the fridge for up to a week or in the freezer for 6 months.

Chicken Stock

Makes about 1.5 litres

1 chicken carcass (from a roast chicken)

2 carrots, broken in half

1 onion, quartered

2 celery sticks, broken in half

a few peppercorns

2 bay leaves

1. Put the chicken carcass in a large saucepan. Cover it with at least 1.5 litres of water and bring the water to the boil. Skim off any starchy brown foam that collects on the surface of the liquid and keep skimming until the foam is white.

2. Add the vegetables, peppercorns and bay leaves. Turn the heat down very low and simmer for about 2 hours until you have a light brown stock. Strain the liquid through a fine sieve into a container.

3. The stock can be used immediately, but if you want to remove any fat, leave the stock in the fridge overnight. The fat will harden and collect at the top and is then easily skimmed off. This stock keeps well in the fridge for up to a week or in the freezer for 3 months.

Nutritional Information

On the following pages you will find nutritional details for the recipes in the book. We've made these as exact as possible but they may vary slightly depending on the ingredients you use when you cook the dish. The figures are per serving unless otherwise specified. Optional ingredients are not included in the analysis.

Kcals Kilocalories refer to the calories, or energy, in food. The calorie counts here are all in kcals. Kj (kilojoules) are just a different way of measuring energy and are not something we list here.

Protein Everyone needs protein for the growth and repair of tissues in the body, and meat, poultry, fish, eggs, dairy, nuts and pulses are all good sources. Research suggests that protein can help you feel fuller for longer.

Carbs Unrefined, wholegrain, low GI carbs such as wholewheat flour, brown rice and pulses are an important part of our diet, even when trying to lose weight.

Sugar This means the total sugar in food, which includes the natural sugars in fruit, vegetables, milk and yoghurt. It's the free sugars – sugar added to food – that we need to cut back on.

Fat The figures for fat means the total fat content, including monounsaturated and polyunsaturated fats and saturated fat. Monounsaturated fats are found in nuts and seeds, olive and rapeseed oil, and polyunsaturated fats in oily fish and vegetable oils. They are healthier types of fat but are still high in calories.

Saturated fats are found in foods such as fatty cuts of meat, butter and cheese. A diet high in saturated fat has been shown to increase the risk of heart disease.

Fibre This is found in plant foods and cannot be completely broken down by digestion. Foods such as fruit, vegetables, nuts, seeds and pulses, as well as cereals like wheat, rice, maize, corn and barley, all contain fibre. When cereals are refined some of the fibre is removed.

Salt The figures given are based on the ingredients in the recipe but do not include salt added as seasoning to taste. A high salt intake is linked with high blood pressure.

The following table shows the recommended daily amount of these various nutrients for different calorie intakes. These figures are guidelines, NOT a target.

Kcals	2,500 kcals	2,000 kcals	1,400 kcals	1,200 kcals
Protein (g)	55	45	45	45
Carbs (g)	300	270	190	160
Sugar (g)	120	90	63	54
Fat (g)	90	70	49	42
Saturated fat (g)	30	20	14	12
Fibre (g)	30	30	30	30
Salt (g)	6	6	6	6

Savoury French Toast

Page 19
Kcals 335
Protein (g) 19
Carbs (g) 21
Sugar (g) 6
Fat (g) 19
Sat fat (g) 9
Fibre (g) 3
Salt (g) 1

Oat Pancakes with Apple Compote

Page 21
Kcals 390
Protein (g) 12
Carbs (g) 45
Sugar (g) 14
Fat (g) 17
Sat fat (g) 7.5
Fibre (g) 6
Salt (g) 0.9

Classic French Omelette

Page 23
Kcals 278
Protein (g) 23
Carbs (g) 0
Sugar (g) 0
Fat (g) 21
Sat fat (g) 7
Fibre (g) 0
Salt (g) 0.8

Rolled Omelette

Page 24
Kcals 290
Protein (g) 25
Carbs (g) 0.7
Sugar (g) 0
Fat (g) 20.5
Sat fat (g) 6
Fibre (g) 0.8
Salt (g) 1.4

Baked Eggs with Chorizo and Peppers

Page 26
Kcals 244
Protein (g) 17
Carbs (g) 9
Sugar (g) 8
Fat (g) 15
Sat fat (g) 5
Fibre (g) 2.5
Salt (g) 1.2

Huevos Rancheros

Page 28
Kcals 524
Protein (g) 22
Carbs (g) 49
Sugar (g) 13
Fat (g) 24.5
Sat fat (g) 8.5
Fibre (g) 10
Salt (g) 1

Sweet Potato and Black Bean Fritters

Page 31
Kcals 286
Protein (g) 9
Carbs (g) 45
Sugar (g) 9
Fat (g) 5
Sat fat (g) 1
Fibre (g) 11
Salt (g) 0.2

Tacos

Page 32
Kcals 534
Protein (g) 14
Carbs (g) 61
Sugar (g) 4.5
Fat (g) 24
Sat fat (g) 5
Fibre (g) 8
Salt (g) 1

Stuffed Eggs

Page 34
Kcals 125 (per egg)
Protein (g) 11
Carbs (g) 0.7
Sugar (g) 0.6
Fat (g) 9
Sat fat (g) 3.5
Fibre (g) 0
Salt (g) 0.5

Apple Soda Bread

Page 37
Kcals 186 (per slice)
Protein (g) 5
Carbs (g) 38
Sugar (g) 6.5
Fat (g) 1
Sat fat (g) 0.5
Fibre (g) 2
Salt (g) 0.7

Sweetcorn and Asparagus Soup

Page 40
Kcals 225
Protein (g) 28
Carbs (g) 14
Sugar (g) 6
Fat (g) 6
Sat fat (g) 1
Fibre (g) 4
Salt (g) 1.1

Pesto and Mozzarella Rolls

Page 43
Kcals 264 (per roll)
Protein (g) 10
Carbs (g) 28
Sugar (g) 1
Fat (g) 11
Sat fat (g) 4
Fibre (g) 4
Salt (g) 0.3

Calzone

Page 44
Kcals 499
Protein (g) 22.5
Carbs (g) 45
Sugar (g) 4
Fat (g) 23
Sat fat (g) 11
Fibre (g) 7
Salt (g) 0.96

Nutty Noodle Salad

Page 47
Kcals 479
Protein (g) 30
Carbs (g) 54
Sugar (g) 6
Fat (g) 14
Sat fat (g) 3
Fibre (g) 6
Salt (g) 2.9

Falafel Scotch Eggs

Page 48
Kcals 332
Protein (g) 14
Carbs (g) 20
Sugar (g) 2
Fat (g) 21
Sat fat (g) 3.5
Fibre (g) 4
Salt (g) 0.4

White Bean Salad

Page 50
Kcals 275
Protein (g) 21
Carbs (g) 25
Sugar (g) 5
Fat (g) 8
Sat fat (g) 1
Fibre (g) 11
Salt (g) 0.6

Roast Squash Salad with Feta

Page 53
Kcals 306
Protein (g) 13
Carbs (g) 36
Sugar (g) 11.5
Fat (g) 11
Sat fat (g) 7
Fibre (g) 6
Salt (g) 1.3

Freekeh and Goat's Cheese Salad

Page 54
Kcals 273
Protein (g) 8
Carbs (g) 35
Sugar (g) 17
Fat (g) 10
Sat fat (g) 3
Fibre (g) 7
Salt (g) 0.7

Pasta and Chickpeas

Page 57
Kcals 390
Protein (g) 16
Carbs (g) 44
Sugar (g) 4
Fat (g) 14
Sat fat (g) 3
Fibre (g) 10
Salt (g) 0.9

Quinoa and Chorizo Salad

Page 58
Kcals 270
Protein (g) 12
Carbs (g) 18
Sugar (g) 5
Fat (g) 16
Sat fat (g) 4
Fibre (g) 4
Salt (g) 0.9

Celeriac and Lentil Salad

Page 60
Kcals 133
Protein (g) 7
Carbs (g) 15
Sugar (g) 7
Fat (g) 3
Sat fat (g) 0.5
Fibre (g) 7.5
Salt (g) 0.2

Pea and Ricotta Dip

Page 62
Kcals 152
Protein (g) 8
Carbs (g) 7
Sugar (g) 2
Fat (g) 10
Sat fat (g) 3
Fibre (g) 3
Salt (g) 0.2

Chicken on Little Gems

Page 64
Kcals 150
Protein (g) 23
Carbs (g) 7
Sugar (g) 6
Fat (g) 3
Sat fat (g) 1
Fibre (g) 2
Salt (g) 0.6

Grilled Chicken, Asparagus and Courgette Salad

Page 67
Kcals 183
Protein (g) 21
Carbs (g) 2.5
Sugar (g) 2.5
Fat (g) 10
Sat fat (g) 1.5
Fibre (g) 1.5
Salt (g) 0.2

Chicken Drumsticks

Page 69
Kcals 274
Protein (g) 35
Carbs (g) 0
Sugar (g) 0
Fat (g) 15
Sat fat (g) 3.5
Fibre (g) 0.5
Salt (g) 0.43

Coleslaw

Page 69
Kcals 66
Protein (g) 1.5
Carbs (g) 4
Sugar (g) 3.5
Fat (g) 4.5
Sat fat (g) 1
Fibre (g) 2
Salt (g) trace

Summer Minestrone

Page 72
Kcals 208
Protein (g) 14
Carbs (g) 15
Sugar (g) 12
Fat (g) 8
Sat fat (g) 3
Fibre (g) 8.5
Salt (g) 0.2

Winter Minestrone

Page 75
Kcals 212
Protein (g) 15
Carbs (g) 20
Sugar (g) 11
Fat (g) 6
Sat fat (g) 1
Fibre (g) 12
Salt (g) 0.2

Mushroom Noodle Soup

Page 77
Kcals 125
Protein (g) 4.5
Carbs (g) 22
Sugar (g) 4
Fat (g) 1.5
Sat fat (g) 0.5
Fibre (g) 2
Salt (g) 1.7

Chicken Harira

Page 78
Kcals 387
Protein (g) 44
Carbs (g) 18
Sugar (g) 8
Fat (g) 14.5
Sat fat (g) 3.5
Fibre (g) 5
Salt (g) 0.7

My Carbonara

Page 81
Kcals 436
Protein (g) 22
Carbs (g) 42
Sugar (g) 3
Fat (g) 18
Sat fat (g) 7
Fibre (g) 8
Salt (g) 1.1

Miso-braised Aubergines

Page 82
Kcals 104
Protein (g) 2
Carbs (g) 7
Sugar (g) 5
Fat (g) 7
Sat fat (g) 1
Fibre (g) 4
Salt (g) 0.2

Thai Vegetable Curry

Page 84
Kcals about 317
Protein (g) 7
Carbs (g) 30
Sugar (g) 10
Fat (g) 18
Sat fat (g) 15
Fibre (g) 6
Salt (g) 1.6

Cauliflower and Broccoli Salad

Page 87
Kcals 454
Protein (g) 19
Carbs (g) 13
Sugar (g) 5
Fat (g) 33
Sat fat (g) 4.5
Fibre (g) 11
Salt (g) trace

American-style Squash Chilli

Page 89
Kcals 174
Protein (g) 6
Carbs (g) 23
Sugar (g) 16
Fat (g) 4
Sat fat (g) 1
Fibre (g) 10
Salt (g) 0.6

Sweetcorn and Bacon Cornbread

Page 90
Kcals 135 (per square)
Protein (g) 6
Carbs (g) 18
Sugar (g) 2
Fat (g) 4
Sat fat (g) 1
Fibre (g) 1.5
Salt (g) 0.5

Fish with Lemon and Orange Butter Sauce

Page 93
Kcals 337
Protein (g) 30
Carbs (g) 1
Sugar (g) 1
Fat (g) 24
Sat fat (g) 7.5
Fibre (g) 0
Salt (g) 0.4

Greek Baked Prawns

Page 94
Kcals 323
Protein (g) 27
Carbs (g) 8
Sugar (g) 7
Fat (g) 21
Sat fat (g) 11
Fibre (g) 2
Salt (g) 2.2

Prawn Pilaf

Page 96
Kcals 395
Protein (g) 30
Carbs (g) 51
Sugar (g) 4
Fat (g) 6.5
Sat fat (g) 1
Fibre (g) 5
Salt (g) 1.5

Roasted Fish with Lime Tartare

Page 98
Kcals 317
Protein (g) 29
Carbs (g) 4
Sugar (g) 1
Fat (g) 21
Sat fat (g) 10
Fibre (g) 0.5
Salt (g) 0.7

Trout and Watercress Salad

Page 101
Kcals 290
Protein (g) 34
Carbs (g) 6
Sugar (g) 6
Fat (g) 13
Sat fat (g) 2
Fibre (g) 2.5
Salt (g) 2

Skate Wings with Salsa Verde

Page 102
Kcals 349
Protein (g) 42
Carbs (g) 4
Sugar (g) 4
Fat (g) 11
Sat fat (g) 2
Fibre (g) 1
Salt (g) 2.5

Mediterranean Fish Casserole

Page 104
Kcals 234
Protein (g) 25
Carbs (g) 15
Sugar (g) 4.5
Fat (g) 7
Sat fat (g) 1
Fibre (g) 4
Salt (g) 0.5

Penne and Sausage Bake

Page 107
Kcals 526
Protein (g) 23
Carbs (g) 35
Sugar (g) 8
Fat (g) 31
Sat fat (g) 13
Fibre (g) 8
Salt (g) 1.9

Chicken Stir-fry

Page 109
Kcals 254
Protein (g) 39
Carbs (g) 8
Sugar (g) 4
Fat (g) 7
Sat fat (g) 1
Fibre (g) 4
Salt (g) 1.4

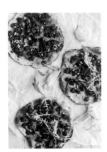

Lamb Flatbreads

Page 110
Kcals 311
Protein (g) 18
Carbs (g) 30
Sugar (g) 5
Fat (g) 12
Sat fat (g) 4
Fibre (g) 4
Salt (g) 0.7

Lamb and Chickpea Salad

Page 112
Kcals 211
Protein (g) 17
Carbs (g) 12
Sugar (g) 3
Fat (g) 10
Sat fat (g) 3
Fibre (g) 4
Salt (g) 0.2

Beef and Mushroom Stir-fry

Page 114
Kcals 400
Protein (g) 26
Carbs (g) 52
Sugar (g) 4
Fat (g) 8
Sat fat (g) 2
Fibre (g) 6
Salt (g) 1

Simple Dal (with onion garnish)

Page 119
Kcals 281 (345)
Protein (g) 16 (16)
Carbs (g) 36 (39)
Sugar (g) 4 (6)
Fat (g) 7 (12)
Sat fat (g) 0.5 (1)
Fibre (g) 5 (6)
Salt (g) trace

Italian-style Meat Sauce

Page 120
Kcals 181
Protein (g) 16
Carbs (g) 12
Sugar (g) 6
Fat (g) 4
Sat fat (g) 1.5
Fibre (g) 4.5
Salt (g) 0.4

Tomato Sauce

Page 123
Kcals 91 (per 150ml)
Protein (g) 3
Carbs (g) 9
Sugar (g) 8
Fat (g) 4.5
Sat fat (g) 1
Fibre (g) 2
Salt (g) trace

Barley Risotto

Page 124
Kcals 355
Protein (g) 14
Carbs (g) 50
Sugar (g) 5
Fat (g) 10
Sat fat (g) 4
Fibre (g) 5
Salt (g) 2.3

Vegan Baked Beans

Page 126
Kcals 444
Protein (g) 22
Carbs (g) 60
Sugar (g) 14
Fat (g) 8
Sat fat (g) 1
Fibre (g) 23
Salt (g) 0.3

Chickpea and Chard Curry

Page 129
Kcals 354
Protein (g) 13
Carbs (g) 27
Sugar (g) 8
Fat (g) 19
Sat fat (g) 15
Fibre (g) 13
Salt (g) 0.4

Pot-roast Chicken

Page 130
Kcals 510
Protein (g) 55
Carbs (g) 29
Sugar (g) 7
Fat (g) 12
Sat fat (g) 3
Fibre (g) 8
Salt (g) 0.5

Chicken Fried Rice

Page 133
Kcals 400
Protein (g) 26
Carbs (g) 51
Sugar (g) 5
Fat (g) 9
Sat fat (g) 2
Fibre (g) 5
Salt (g) 1.2

Chicken Soup

Page 134
Kcals 270
Protein (g) 20
Carbs (g) 12
Sugar (g) 5
Fat (g) 14
Sat fat (g) 7.5
Fibre (g) 4.5
Salt (g) 0.2

Lamb Keema Peas

Page 136
Kcals 415
Protein (g) 33
Carbs (g) 28
Sugar (g) 10
Fat (g) 17
Sat fat (g) 7
Fibre (g) 8.5
Salt (g) 0.3

Pumpkin Gnocchi with Spinach

Page 140
Kcals 355
Protein (g) 16
Carbs (g) 27
Sugar (g) 3
Fat (g) 19
Sat fat (g) 7
Fibre (g) 6
Salt (g) 1

Spinach and Ricotta Lasagne

Page 142
Kcals 492
Protein (g) 24
Carbs (g) 35
Sugar (g) 10
Fat (g) 26
Sat fat (g) 13
Fibre (g) 9
Salt (g) 2.3

Mushroom Cobbler

Page 145
Kcals 422
Protein (g) 13
Carbs (g) 39
Sugar (g) 6
Fat (g) 17
Sat fat (g) 9
Fibre (g) 10
Salt (g) 0.9

Slow-braised Squid

Page 146
Kcals 343
Protein (g) 27
Carbs (g) 27
Sugar (g) 5
Fat (g) 8
Sat fat (g) 2
Fibre (g) 5
Salt (g) 0.4

Marinated Salmon with Brown Rice

Page 148
Kcals 588
Protein (g) 39
Carbs (g) 41
Sugar (g) 3
Fat (g) 29
Sat fat (g) 5
Fibre (g) 4
Salt (g) 0.4

Mediterranean Chicken Skewers

Page 151
Kcals 145 (per skewer)
Protein (g) 24
Carbs (g) 4
Sugar (g) 3
Fat (g) 3
Sat fat (g) 1
Fibre (g) 1.5
Salt (g) 0.24

Mediterranean Vegetables

Page 153
Kcals 237
Protein (g) 7
Carbs (g) 44
Sugar (g) 16
Fat (g) 1
Sat fat (g) 0.5
Fibre (g) 11
Salt (g) trace

Chicken Meatballs with Couscous and Creamy Tomato Sauce

Page 154
Kcals 555
Protein (g) 33
Carbs (g) 37
Sugar (g) 30
Fat (g) 30
Sat fat (g) 12.5
Fibre (g) 3
Salt (g) 1.4

Chicken Curry

Page 157
Kcals 260
Protein (g) 35
Carbs (g) 6
Sugar (g) 5
Fat (g) 11
Sat fat (g) 6
Fibre (g) 0.5
Salt (g) 0.7

Sausage Casserole (with beans)

Page 158
Kcals 476 (547)
Protein (g) 25 (29)
Carbs (g) 11 (21)
Sugar (g) 10 (10)
Fat (g) 31 (31)
Sat fat (g) 10 (10.5)
Fibre (g) 6 (10)
Salt (g) 1.5 (1.5)

Marinated Lamb with Cauliflower Couscous

Page 161
Kcals 457
Protein (g) 36
Carbs (g) 10
Sugar (g) 7.5
Fat (g) 30
Sat fat (g) 8
Fibre (g) 4
Salt (g) 0.3

Mediterranean Shoulder of Lamb

Page 162
Kcals 639
Protein (g) 71
Carbs (g) 24
Sugar (g) 4
Fat (g) 27
Sat fat (g) 11
Fibre (g) 10
Salt (g) 0.8

Spiced Banana Bread

Page 166
Kcals 164 (per slice)
Protein (g) 15
Carbs (g) 27
Sugar (g) 13.5
Fat (g) 2.5
Sat fat (g) 0.6
Fibre (g) 3.5
Salt (g) trace

Peaches and Raspberries

Page 168
Kcals 219
Protein (g) 3.5
Carbs (g) 14
Sugar (g) 14
Fat (g) 15.5
Sat fat (g) 9
Fibre (g) 5
Salt (g) trace

Banana and Peanut Butter Ice Cream (with choc sauce)

Page 171
Kcals 151 (321)
Protein (g) 3 (5)
Carbs (g) 24 (50)
Sugar (g) 21 (36.5)
Fat (g) 4 (15)
Sat fat (g) 0.8 (7.8)
Fibre (g) 2 (2)
Salt (g) trace

Watermelon, Clementine and Strawberry Granita

Page 172
Kcals 50
Protein (g) 1
Carbs (g) 10
Sugar (g) 10
Fat (g) 0
Sat fat (g) 0
Fibre (g) 2
Salt (g) 0

Frozen Fruit

Page 175
Kcals about 132
Protein (g) 1.5
Carbs (g) 28
Sugar (g) 28
Fat (g) 0
Sat fat (g) 0
Fibre (g) 4.5
Salt (g) 0

Fig Rolls

Page 177 (per biscuit)
Kcals 166
Protein (g) 3
Carbs (g) 17
Sugar (g) 10
Fat (g) 9
Sat fat (g) 4.5
Fibre (g) 3
Salt (g) 0.2

Chocolate and Coconut Biscuits

Page 178
Kcals 170 (per biscuit)
Protein (g) 2
Carbs (g) 11
Sugar (g) 5
Fat (g) 13
Sat fat (g) 9
Fibre (g) 3
Salt (g) 0.2

Apple and Carrot Steamed Puddings

Page 180
Kcals 165
Protein (g) 6.5
Carbs (g) 27
Sugar (g) 6.5
Fat (g) 2.5
Sat fat (g) 1
Fibre (g) 3.5
Salt (g) 0.7

Pear and Blueberry Galette

Page 182
Kcals 420
Protein (g) 6
Carbs (g) 27
Sugar (g) 10
Fat (g) 26
Sat fat (g) 16
Fibre (g) 6.6
Salt (g) trace

Blackberry and Apple Crumble

Page 184
Kcals 325
Protein (g) 5.5
Carbs (g) 38
Sugar (g) 16.5
Fat (g) 14.5
Sat fat (g) 6.5
Fibre (g) 8
Salt (g) 0.2

Pineapple and Grapefruit Salad with Coconut Cream

Page 187
Kcals 275
Protein (g) 2.5
Carbs (g) 25
Sugar (g) 24
Fat (g) 17
Sat fat (g) 15
Fibre (g) 4.5
Salt (g) trace

Lime Sandwich Cake

Page 188
Kcals 267 (per slice)
Protein (g) 3.8
Carbs (g) 21
Sugar (g) 11
Fat (g) 18
Sat fat (g) 11
Fibre (g) 1.8
Salt (g) trace

Green Pesto

Page 192
Kcals 70
Protein (g) 2.5
Carbs (g) 0.5
Sugar (g) 0
Fat (g) 6.5
Sat fat (g) 1.5
Fibre (g) 0
Salt (g) trace

Red Pesto

Page 192
Kcals 103
Protein (g) 2.5
Carbs (g) 4
Sugar (g) 4,5
Fat (g) 8
Sat fat (g) 1,5
Fibre (g) 2
Salt (g) 0.7

Raw Tomato Salsa

Page 193
Kcals 19
Protein (g) 0.5
Carbs (g) 3.5
Sugar (g) 3
Fat (g) 0
Sat fat (g) 0
Fibre (g) 1
Salt (g) trace

Mint and Yoghurt Sauce

Page 193
Kcals 57
Protein (g) 4
Carbs (g) 5
Sugar (g) 5
Fat (g) 2
Sat fat (g) 1
Fibre (g) 0.5
Salt (g) trace

Mayonnaise

Page 196
Kcals 117 (per 15g tbsp)
Protein (g) 0.3
Carbs (g) 0
Sugar (g) 0
Fat (g) 14
Sat fat (g) 2.5
Fibre (g) 0
Salt (g) trace

Roasted Red Peppers

Page 196
Kcals 39 (per pepper)
Protein (g) 1
Carbs (g) 6
Sugar (g) 6
Fat (g) 3
Sat fat (g) 0.5
Fibre (g) 3
Salt (g) 0

Corn Tortillas

Page 197
Kcals 73 (per tortilla)
Protein (g) 2
Carbs (g) 15
Sugar (g) 1
Fat (g) 0
Sat fat (g) 0
Fibre (g) 0.5
Salt (g) 0

My 5-Week Plan

When you're keen to lose weight, having a plan to follow can be a real help. You don't have to think too hard – just follow my suggestions and you're sure of having plenty of delicious food but not too many calories.

It's fine to swap some of the meals in the plan for your own favourite recipes, but make sure you keep your menu based on plenty of vegetables and some protein and choose unrefined carbs and good fats. This is not a crash plan. It is designed to help you have a healthy diet, while cutting right back on added sugar and empty calories. It also helps to keep your blood sugar steady.

If you do change dishes, try to choose ones with a similar calorie count, but a few calories more or less each day isn't going to ruin your diet. And you can have as many green and non-starchy vegetables as you like, so add what you want and they'll help to fill you up. We've suggested salads and vegetable accompaniments for some dishes but feel free to include more. Most of these meals are fine for the non-dieters in the family, but you'll probably want to do some extra side dishes for them – perhaps some wholewheat toast or oatcakes with the soups, and brown rice or sweet potato with some of the main dishes. Non-dieters can have more of the yummy cakes and puddings too!

While you're following the plan it's important to drink plenty of water. Water helps to fill you up and reduces the urge to snack or overeat, which is really helpful! You can have tea and coffee – no sugar – but avoid sweet sodas, even the calorie-free ones. The aim of this plan to retrain your taste buds to enjoy the natural flavours of food and wean yourself off the sweet stuff. Alcohol contains loads of calories so best to stay off it for these five weeks too.

Here's what to do:

Week 1   Aim for 1,400 kcals a day. That works out to an average of about 300 kcals for breakfast, 350 for lunch and 550 for your evening meal, plus two snacks on weekdays.

Week 2   Aim for 1,300 kcals a day. That works out to an average of about 300 kcals for breakfast, 300 for lunch and 500 for your evening meal, plus two snacks on weekdays.

Weeks 3, 4, 5   Aim for 1,200 kcals a day. That works out to an average of about 250 kcals for breakfast, 300 for lunch and 450 for your evening meal, plus two snacks on weekdays.

We thought you might enjoy a slightly bigger breakfast at the weekends or a special supper, so we've dropped the snacks on the Saturday and Sunday menus to allow for more calories at the other meals.

Week 1

	BREAKFAST	SNACK	LUNCH	SNACK	EVENING MEAL
MONDAY	2 boiled eggs + slice wholemeal toast	2 satsumas	Trout and watercress salad + 50g wholemeal bread roll	1 oatcake + raw tomato salsa	Chicken meatballs with couscous and creamy tomato sauce
TUESDAY	Savoury French toast	1 medium banana	Chicken fried rice	50g hummus + raw veg sticks	My carbonara
WEDNESDAY	1 x 125g pot of yoghurt + 200g mango	20g almonds	Vegan baked beans	1 medium pear	Skate wings with salsa verde Peaches and raspberries
THURSDAY	Classic French omelette	2 medium kiwi	Mushroom noodle soup	1 medium apple	Marinated lamb with cauli couscous Blackberry and apple crumble
FRIDAY	Porridge with raspberries	2 medium kiwi	Celeriac and lentil salad	1 x 125g pot of yoghurt	Beef and mushroom stir-fry Pear and blueberry galette
SATURDAY	Tacos		Baked eggs with chorizo and peppers		Prawn pilaf Pineapple and grapefruit salad with coconut cream
SUNDAY	Huevos rancheros		White bean salad		Pot-roast chicken Apple and carrot steamed puddings

Week 2

	BREAKFAST	SNACK	LUNCH	SNACK	EVENING MEAL
MONDAY	Apple soda bread, lightly spread with butter	2 satsumas	Lamb and chickpea salad	20g almonds	Sausage casserole + 80g steamed broccoli
TUESDAY	2 boiled eggs + slice wholemeal toast	1 x 125g pot of yoghurt	Mediterranean chicken skewers + green salad	1 slice of spiced banana bread	Marinated salmon with brown rice
WEDNESDAY	Sweet potato and black bean fritters	1 medium banana	Winter minestrone + 50g wholemeal roll	2 medium kiwi	Chicken harira + 80g broccoli Banana and peanut butter ice cream
THURSDAY	Half a grapefruit + scrambled eggs (2 eggs, 1 tsp butter) + slice wholemeal toast	2 medium kiwi	Celeriac and lentil salad	2 satsumas	Fish with lemon and orange butter sauce + 100g new potatoes + 80g green beans Pear and blueberry galette
FRIDAY	3 heaped tbsp muesli + 150ml milk + handful raspberries	2 satsumas	Freekeh and goat's cheese salad	50g hummus + raw veg sticks	Thai vegetable curry + 50g brown rice (raw wt)
SATURDAY	Oat pancakes with apple compote		Chicken on little gems		Mediterranean shoulder of lamb + green veg Apple and carrot steamed puddings
SUNDAY	Savoury French toast		Barley risotto		Lamb keema peas + wholemeal pitta Frozen fruit

Week 3

	BREAKFAST	SNACK	LUNCH	SNACK	EVENING MEAL
MONDAY	1 x 125g pot of yoghurt + 200g mango	1 medium orange	Falafel Scotch egg + green salad	20g almonds	Sausage casserole
TUESDAY	Classic French omelette	1 medium banana	Simple dal	1 pear	Chicken harira + green salad
WEDNESDAY	Poached egg on 1 slice of wholemeal toast	2 satsumas	Pasta and chickpeas	1 apple	Greek baked prawns Peaches and raspberries
THURSDAY	Porridge + handful of blueberries	1 apple	Summer minestrone	20g almonds	My carbonara
FRIDAY	Apple soda bread, lightly spread with butter	20g almonds	White bean salad	1 medium banana	Chicken fried rice 2 medium kiwi
SATURDAY	Huevos rancheros		Roast squash salad with feta		Roasted fish with lime tartare + green veg
SUNDAY	Savoury French toast		Mediterranean fish casserole		Marinated lamb with cauliflower couscous

Week 4

	BREAKFAST	SNACK	LUNCH	SNACK	EVENING MEAL
MONDAY	1 slice wholemeal toast + 2 tsp peanut butter + 1 banana	1 apple	Quinoa and chorizo salad	1 x 125g pot of yoghurt	Pasta and chickpeas + green salad
TUESDAY	Porridge + handful of blueberries	2 satsumas	Pea and ricotta dip + 2 slices wholemeal toast	20g almonds	Beef and mushroom stir-fry
WEDNESDAY	Half a grapefruit + scrambled eggs (2 eggs, 1 tsp butter) + 1 slice wholemeal toast	1 x 125g pot of yoghurt	Sweetcorn and asparagus soup	50g hummus + raw veg sticks	Chicken curry + 40g brown rice (raw wt)
THURSDAY	1 x 125g pot of yoghurt + 1 banana	1 pear	Roast squash salad with feta	50g hummus + raw veg sticks	Spinach and ricotta lasagne
FRIDAY	Classic French omelette	1 kiwi	Trout and watercress salad	100g pomegranate	Sausage casserole + green salad
SATURDAY	2 boiled eggs + slice wholemeal toast		Tacos		Lamb keema peas
SUNDAY	Oat pancakes with apple compote		Cauliflower and broccoli salad		Fish with lemon and orange butter sauce + green veg

Week 5

	BREAKFAST	SNACK	LUNCH	SNACK	EVENING MEAL
MONDAY	2 boiled eggs + slice wholemeal toast	100g pomegranate	Freekeh and goat's cheese salad	1 apple	Marinated salmon with brown rice
TUESDAY	Scrambled eggs (2 eggs + 1 tsp butter) + 30g smoked salmon	1 kiwi	Vegan baked beans	1 orange	Mushroom cobbler + 80g green beans
WEDNESDAY	1 slice wholemeal toast + 2 tsp peanut butter + 1 banana	1 apple	Lamb flatbreads	20g almonds	Pumpkin gnocchi with spinach + green salad
THURSDAY	Classic French omelette	1 oatcake + raw tomato salsa	Chickpea and chard curry	1 plum	Calzone + green salad
FRIDAY	Half a grapefruit + scrambled eggs (2 eggs, 1 tsp butter) + 1 slice wholemeal toast	1 orange	Nutty noodle salad	1 apple	Beef and mushroom stir-fry
SATURDAY	Huevos rancheros		Mushroom noodle soup		Spinach and ricotta lasagne
SUNDAY	Tacos		Quinoa and chorizo salad		Marinated lamb with cauliflower couscous

More bestsellers from Davina . . .

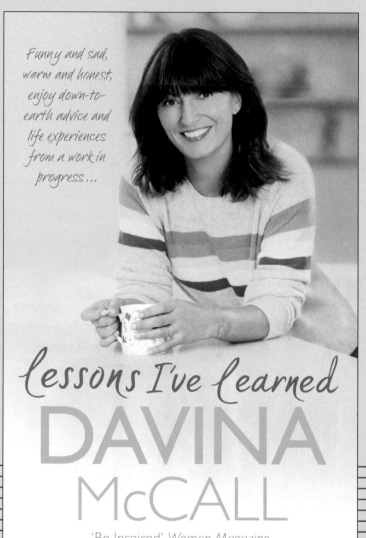

Funny and sad,
warm and honest,
enjoy down-to-
earth advice and
life experiences
from a work in
progress...

lessons I've learned

DAVINA
McCALL

'Be Inspired' *Woman Magazine*

Davina's
5 WEEKS TO
SUGAR-FREE

Yummy, easy recipes to help you kick sugar and feel amazing

Eat carbs and still **lose weight**
with my AMAZING 5 week SMART CARB PLAN!

Davina's
SMART CARBS

Seven Dials:
Fresh Publishing, Timeless Books

The delicious follow-up to No.1 bestseller *DAVINA'S 5 WEEKS TO SUGAR-FREE*

Davina's
SUGAR-FREE
IN A HURRY

The smart and fast way to eat less sugar and feel fab!

Index

Thanks All!!

First off, hugest thanks to the wonderful Catherine Phipps for developing another bunch of the yummiest most delicious recipes. You are incredible.

Thanks to the amazing Elisabeth Hoff for the pictures of me. You are the best of the best and I love working with you. And to Angie Smith, Cheryl Phelps-Gardiner and Michael Douglas – love you lots and big hugs for helping me look and feel lovely . . . please can you all come and live with me so I can look like that every day?!!!

Debby Lewis-Harrison took some great pics of the food which make my mouth water. Thanks to her and to the food-styling team – Emily Jonzen, Nicola Roberts, Tonia Shuttleworth and Ruth Ferrier. Once again, Helen Ewing and Abi Hartshorne have made the book look totally gorgeous, and thank you too to the Orion production people – Fiona McIntosh and Katie Horrocks – for bringing it all together.

Thank you Fiona Hunter for a great job with nutritional info and advice, and Elise See Tai and Vicki Robinson for expert proofreading and indexing.

Amanda . . . you are beautiful. Inside and out. You have a captivating and beautiful energy. Thank you for everything, I hope you know how very grateful I am.

Jinny . . . you are like a mother hen. I don't know where I'd be without you . . . thank you for your love and diligence 🖤

Mary, Clare, Emily and Hayley . . . and Georgie and Blaise and all the gang at James Grant, I love you guys. No, but I really do. Really really . . .

and as for you Rowan . . . extra special 'mummy' hug for you!

And finally, this is for my kids . . . Chester, for always being willing to try something new! Tilly for always helping me tidy away! And Holly, my vegan, helping us discover amazing tasty vegan food . . . I love you all 😍

lots of love

I'd like to dedicate this book to my children for making me always want to be a better cook,
to Tilly and Holly for showing me that vegan food can be so amazing, and to Sarah. You are my person.

First published in Great Britain in 2018
by Seven Dials, an imprint of the Orion Publishing Group Ltd
Carmelite House, 50 Victoria Embankment
London EC4Y 0DZ
An Hachette UK Company

10 9 8 7 6 5 4 3 2 1

Text © Davina McCall 2018
Design and layout © Orion 2018

A CIP catalogue record for this book is available from
the British Library.

ISBN: 978 1 4091 7570 4

Food director: Catherine Phipps
Food photography: Debby Lewis-Harrison
Portrait photography: Elisabeth Hoff
Art direction: Helen Ewing, Ruth Ferrier
Design: Hart Studio
Project editor: Jinny Johnson
Food stylist: Emily Jonzen
Food stylist's assistant: Nicola Roberts
Props stylist: Tonia Shuttleworth
Proofreader: Elise See Tai
Indexer: Vicki Robinson

Nutritional advice and analysis: Fiona Hunter,
Bsc (Hons) Nutrition, Dip Dietetics

Printed and bound in Germany

Note: While every effort has been made to ensure that the information in this
book is correct, it should not be substituted for medical advice. The recipes
in this book should be used in combination with a healthy lifestyle. If you are
concerned about any aspect of your health, speak to your GP. People under
medical supervision should not come off their medication without speaking to
their health professional.

For more delicious recipes plus
exclusive competitions and sneak
previews from Orion's cookery
writers visit **kitchentales.co.uk**

Follow us

 @kitchentalesuk

 @kitchentalesuk

 @kitchentalesuk